DISCARDED

From Peterloo to the Crystal Palace

George IV

Victoria aged eleven (after R. T. Lane)

FROM PETERLOO TO
THE CRYSTAL PALACE

R. J. WHITE

HEINEMANN EDUCATIONAL BOOKS
LONDON

Heinemann Educational Books Ltd

LONDON   EDINBURGH   MELBOURNE   TORONTO
AUCKLAND   JOHANNESBURG   SINGAPORE
IBADAN   NAIROBI   HONG KONG   NEW DELHI
KUALA LUMPUR

ISBN 0 435 32941 3

Published by Heinemann Educational Books Ltd
48 Charles Street, London WIX 8AH
Printed in Great Britain by
C. Tinling & Co. Ltd, London and Prescot

Contents

To Lawrence Searson
of Heanor and Codnor, Derbyshire,
loyal friend of a lifetime

Preface

My husband finished this book early this year; he had already fallen seriously ill by the late summer, when the first proofs arrived. He had been collecting materials for some years, in fact ever since the successful publication of *Waterloo to Peterloo*, which was a detailed study of the years 1815–1819, a period he always found intensely interesting, since his early research work under Temperley and Trevelyan.

From Peterloo to the Crystal Palace is not only a continuation of that account of near-catastrophe, but stands on its own, as a story of the wonderful recovery of nerve and strength of the English monarchy and the English people. It also draws together many of R.J.'s special interests. It covers the longer period from 1819–1851, with a panoramic view of the crowded events of the reigns of the sons of George III, to the unexpected apotheosis of his grand-daughter, Victoria. Like his beloved master, Thomas Hardy, R.J. could survey the scene from above – with the spirits of the Years and of Irony and of the Pities – and then suddenly swoop down to the particular; from the great seminal minds who influenced events, such as Bentham and Coleridge, to the little men, glow-worm lights compared with these great beacons, but helping to illuminate the darkness. 'You see that man?', that urgent cry of Hardy's poem 'At Lulworth Cove a Century Back' was always deep in R.J.'s mind, as he strove to make us see Bamford the Weaver marching along the Buxton Road south to see London and the face of Lord Castlereagh; or the quiet Quaker Howitts rejoicing while watching the blaze of Nottingham Castle during the Reform Bill riots.

Again like Hardy, R.J. had a tremendous sense not only of Time, but of Place. Derbyshire where he grew up, in Edwardian times, and Nottingham where he went to school by train every day, was his Wessex, or better his Mercia, where he was in touch with its Victorian past through many old relatives and friends, whom he had heard talking about the Crimean War, or the eccentricities of old clergymen, doctors, and teachers, who sursurvived into his youth. He remembered family talk about D. H. Lawrence and his parents: the old miner father was locally judged to be the better man, after all he had the courage to battle for his living at the coal face: his son was 'mardy', or soft; R.J., although a great admirer of the poet and artist, could see the basic truth of this folk-judgement, as an historian. Not surprisingly therefore these Midland counties and their people have an important part in this book.

R.J. always had from his infancy an overwhelming love of English literature, fostered by his remarkable schoolmaster father, A. J. White. Together they tramped the moors and the dales, talking and quoting their great native literature, particularly that of this favourite part of England. R.J. was proud of the fact that Dr. Johnson was a native of neighbouring Staffordshire and that his bookseller father was born on a small farm just north of Ashbourne. He always hooted thrice on the horn of our small car in greeting as we sped past on our way to Bakewell; just as he always sang as we crossed the Trent. There was Byron at the Abbey so close to Nottingham and also Mary Howitt (author of the nursery favourites 'The Spider and the Fly', and 'The Squirrels') who had seen the great funeral procession bringing the hero's body back from Greece to Nottingham. Finally there were the Baileys, father and son, a self-made man of business, owner of a Nottingham newspaper, and the Poet, whom in his last years R.J. 'discovered'. Philip Bailey was no great poet, but he was a Victorian phenomenon, a testimony to the real Victorian love of literature and of the results of hard work, which allowed Bailey (like the great Browning and Tennyson) to live well as a professional poet, either through the generosity of the public, or his father.

So to the triumphant ending at the book with Joseph Paxton, who had risen from lowly Derbyshire beginnings to be head-gardener to the greatest Derbyshire magnate, the oddly named Duke of Devonshire, and to use his own designs for the Lily Conservatories at Chatsworth, the 'Palace of the Peak', as the basis for that glass wonder which housed the Great Exhibition. Here were to be seen all the fantastic variety of products, clever, beautiful or monstrous, of that first industrial revolution which had started in the Pennines, with Arkwright's Mills at Cromford. It was a great pity that R.J.'s beloved Derbyshire painter, Joseph Wright of Derby, who had painted the fantastic glittering beauty of the mills and the furnaces, was not alive to paint the Crystal Palace, for he would have been delighted with the shining lights and the trees inside this Victorian 'Cathedral' of Industry. But the book ends on a question-mark – was it a happy ending? Within were masses of happy people drinking ginger pop (a great improvement on Gin Lane) and wanting enlargement of Mind, 'always supposing this tended to the enlargement of pockets, wages, and substantialities' – but what if it did not? Karl Marx was busy writing in the British Museum 'Workers of the World Unite, you have nothing to lose but your Chains!'– which R.J. thought not true of England at least. But, like Thomas Hardy, he could see ghosts – ghosts of the tragedies of Peterloo and the Derbyshire Rising, and among them was Jeremiah Brandreth, stoically standing in his chains, smoking his old pipe, awaiting death on the Derby gallows, along with his men, who had set out to march on Nottingham and secure 'provisions' for their people – victims of a great injustice, which would always haunt English history and that 'time worn' man, the sensitive historian.

4 Storey's Way,   Vera White,
Cambridge.   3rd December 1971.

Acknowledgements

The author and publishers would like to thank the *Radio Times Hulton Picture Library* for permission to reproduce the frontispieces and plates 1, 3, 4, 5, 6, 9, 10 and 13; *The Mansell Collection* for plates 2, 7, 8, 15 and 16; and *The Nottingham Public Library* for plates 11 and 12.

List of Illustrations

CHAPTER I

After Peterloo

THE BATTLE of Peterloo was fought on 9th August, 1819. It was not literally a battle, but what a mealy-mouthed generation prefers to call a 'confrontation'. A small body of the 15th Hussars which fought at Waterloo had clashed with an unarmed crowd of Lancashire weavers and their wives and children in St Peter's Fields, Manchester. Eleven people had been killed and several hundred wounded.

Life went on as well as death. Nearly three months before Peterloo a daughter was born at Kensington Palace to the Duke and Duchess of Kent. One of the child's godfathers was the Tsar Alexander II of Russia, so they called the child Alexandrina. For her second name they called her Victoria, after her mother. The Prince Regent would have liked her to be called Georgina, but the spirit of English history would have none of it, and Victoria she became. She narrowly escaped the tumult of Peterloo, but when she was seven she rode in Windsor Great Park with her uncle, who had become King George IV, an occasion she was to remember all her life.

She herself became Queen in 1837, eighteen years after Peterloo. The years between form an interim period little regarded by historians save in political terms. They call it the Age of the Great Reform Bill, for that great landmark came at its midpoint. When the Bill was passed people like Alfred Tennyson and his sisters at Somersby Rectory rushed out to ring the church bells, as if the nation had been delivered from catastrophe. Perhaps it had, for the threat of civil war had hung over the country for many weeks. In the positive sense however what had happened was nothing very much. Some half a hundred rotten boroughs had been disfranchised and about the same number had been given representation that had not enjoyed it before. A few hundred people, mainly shop-keepers and small professional people known as 'Ten-pound householders', had been given the vote. Among them was Thomas Carlyle who went along and paid his shilling to register the right to enjoy the privilege of helping to elect the members of the 'Talking-shop' or 'National Tongue-Palaver' which were among his names for the House of Commons. It is not true to say that the Reform Act had absolutely nothing to do with the triumph of democracy, for as the Duke of Wellington had said in his prescient way:

> If I say *A* I must say *B,*
> And so go on to *C* and *D* . . .
> And so no end you see there'll be
> If I but once say *A, B, C.*

It was *le premier pas qui coûte.* Once the political nation had been re-defined, it could be re-defined again—and again—in 1867, 1884, 1918 and 1925. Thus the people became sovereign by its own action, step by step, beginning with the concession of a tiny share of its monopoly to a fraction of the middle-class. More important perhaps, the people did it in its own way, which would one day be known as 'the inevitability of gradualness'. That, more than anything else, was what the church-bells rang for in 1832: the triumph of the English way of doing things.

It was a way that had been establishing itself amidst a great deal of national self-consciousness for half a century. Alien and detestable ways like massacre and assassination had been planned, and partially executed, at St Peter's Field in Manchester and in Cato Street, off the Edgware Road, but as Halévy put it 'the gulf which separates the history of modern England from the contemporary history of the European nations' had succeeded in emptying of their significance those two mighty watchwords, Revolution and Reaction, which were so powerful elsewhere.

After the Peterloo 'massacre' and the Cato Street 'assassination-plot', instead of a 'White-Terror' the nation indulged itself in low comic relief at 'The Queen's Trial' for adultery. Queen Caroline had returned from abroad to claim her Royal rank beside the new king, George IV, who had promptly set on foot divorce proceed-

ings in the form of a Bill of Pains and Penalties which he induced
his Ministers to introduce into the House of Lords. The evidence
against the Queen, produced principally by Italians of low repute,
provided sufficient salacious gossip to eclipse the ugly machinations
of Arthur Thistlewood and the would-be assassins of Cato Street,
and the affair in general seems to have done much to restore the
good humour of the nation. The withdrawal of the Bill of Pains
and Penalties, it has been said, saved the State from convulsion.
The chief sufferers were the King's Ministers who had made sorry
fools of themselves by attempting to do the behest of a master like
George IV at the expense of a mistress like his Queen. The whole
business dissolved into a howl of rueful laughter. In the summer
of 1821, shortly after she had been refused admission to Westminster Abbey for the King's Coronation, Caroline died. Scarcely
twelve months later, the best-hated member of the Cabinet died
also when Castlereagh cut his throat. Sidmouth had retired already, to be succeeded as Home Secretary by Peel. With Sidmouth
died the spy-mania that had afflicted the country so frequently
since the end of the war. With Canning in Castlereagh's place,
Peel in Sidmouth's, 'Prosperity' Robinson as Chancellor of the
Exchequer, and Huskisson as President of the Board of Trade, the
era of 'Liberal-Toryism' was dawning. The cast of the Victorian
melodrama was already on the stage. The age of Eldon, 'chaos
and old night', had passed away.

As the dust of Peterloo settled in St Peter's Fields and swords
settled back into scabbards, Lord Grey ('Reform-Bill Grey') wrote
to the Duke of Devonshire that he thought it 'absolutely necessary' that the Whig party should now return to its post as leaders
of the people against the lawless execution of power. Led by Grey
himself, the Whigs had withdrawn from the leadership of reform
politics in the 1790's, many of them even seceding from Parliament as the House of Commons cold-shouldered even the mildest
proposal for reform. They went home, and stayed there, for the
'duration'. The cause of reform wrote the veteran John Horne
Tooke, from his retirement at Wimbledon, was dead and buried.
All the same 'J.C. is a believer in the Resurrection' wrote another
veteran, the game old Major Cartwright. It was men like Cartwright and Cobbett and Burdett who kept hope alive, 'getting

heartily cursed for disturbing the quiet of the country', as the Major said. When the War was over it was still perilous to bear the Parliamentary Reform banner in a world noisy with Hampden Clubs and Luddites and the uproar over Oliver the Spy. When the great reform-rally gathered in St Peter's Fields in the summer of 1819 it was not a Whig gentleman but a Radical demagogue who led it. Henry Hunt, the orator in the white-topper, went to prison for two and a half years, and Sir Francis Burdett got himself fined £2,000 and imprisoned for three months for a libellous letter of protest, and Earl Fitzwilliam got dismissed from his Lord Lieutenancy of the West Riding for joining in. It was his participation with Fitzwilliam that led Earl Grey to explain to the Duke of Devonshire that he declined to give the least countenance to Henry Hunt and his associates even while he was concerned that 'the people' should not 'find themselves abandoned by their natural protectors . . . '. Surely, he protested, the greatest evil to which any country could be exposed, 'is that of a separation between the higher and the lower orders of the community'. Such separation must always be fatal to both peace and liberty, a calamity which is likely to happen whenever an injured people finds itself abandoned by their natural protectors.

Grey expressed himself in terms of the quasi-feudal community that was passing away, wherein one part of society lived under the protection, if not the patronage, of another part; wherein the natural leaders of the people were assumed to be the aristocracy. This was still true but it was becoming less unquestioned. It would remain true for so long as the people failed to produce leaders of their own. This failure was to last for at least another century. To say that this failure coincided with the survival of a 'deferential society' is only to employ sociological jargon, to express in pejorative terms the well-known and obvious fact that men prefer to be led by those who, rightly or wrongly, they imagine to be their 'betters', which means an aristocracy of some kind. So, in the age of the Great Reform Bill, 'the politics of the people' continued to mean what it had always meant, something handed down from above. As Major Cartwright said, from his long experience of what he called 'the lower orders', they preferred to confide the protection of their interests to 'persons of more consideration than themselves', and 'generally evinced a jealous dislike to raise those of their own standing to stations of importance'. He was reluctant that they should even be represented on canvas, as Benjamin Robert Haydon discovered when he waited upon His Lordship in connection with his proposed picture of the great Reform meeting of the Trade Unions at Newhall Hill, Birmingham, in 1832. 'Lord Grey did not speak of the unions as he ought', he records in his diary. 'He seemed to think of them as subjects below my pencil.' Haydon thought his picture showed 'the vast utility of the industrious classes obeying the men of property in the neighbourhood as leaders, instead of wildly wreaking their vengeance on property from ignorance and passion. Surely this is a subject kings and lords ought to protect.' Certainly a stout Church and King man like Haydon had no doubt about it.

Grey was one of the most finely-drawn aristocrats of his time. He even looked it, with his high-pitched nose and the delicacy of bone structure in head and face. His mind and manners were like that too. In the crowd of Radical politicians a man like Grey looked a thoroughbred among draught-horses, which was how Byron described him. 'There's nothing like 'em when they add intelligence to breeding', as Haydon remarked. Besides them, common men went out like candle-flames in strong sunshine. The history of reform politics in the early nineteenth century might be convincingly written from the history of half a dozen aristocratic families, such was their power and influence over the rest of English mankind. To imagine that it could be written as the history of something called 'the working-class' is to submit to an illusion, an undergraduate fantasy lingering in nominally adult minds.

In the reign of George IV there was a high mortality-rate among both poets and politicians. Keats, Byron and Shelley were all dead in comparative youth by 1825. Among the politicians, the archmediocrity, as Disraeli called Lord Liverpool, fell down in a fit in 1827, but when Canning followed him within six months he may be said to have left a gap in nature. He was succeeded by a comparative nonentity known as 'Goody Goderich', a 'transient and embarrassed phantom' who came and went within another six. Then the Duke of Wellington took over and saw George IV out

and William IV in. The rapid turn-over in ministries in the later
'twenties is surpassed only by certain periods of the Third Republic.

If Tory statesmen were in the forefront of the casualties that
was because they were in the forefront of ministerial politics.
After all, the Tories had been in office with little intermission for
thirty years, and now that reform was on the way they remained
in the lead. Properly speaking, England had no Whig Ministry
until Lord Grey assumed office in the first year of William IV's
reign. It is only by reading history backwards, and by imagining
that Whigs and Tories were the counterparts of Liberals and
Conservatives in the time of Gladstone and Disraeli, or in the
early years of the present century, that the contest over the Great
Reform Bill can be read as a straight political fight between Whigs
and Tories. In fact there is a great deal more truth in the remark of
William Hazlitt that Whigs and Tories were the names of two
coaches travelling along the same road in the same direction and
splashing each other with mud as they went. The passengers in
each were diverse—but not all that diverse—collections of upper
and upper-middle class men. Now and then, when a coach got
stuck on a steep hill, as in 1830–32 when trying to carry the load
labelled 'Reform Bill', they would summon the brawny assistance
of peasants and artisans to push them over the last lap, but they
generally went down the other side without looking back. Their
contest was very much a sham-fight. If their backers, or pushers,
threatened to take over the reins, the two vehicles would lock
their wheels and block up the way. No progress could be made
without them, and no progress could be made with them except
in whatever direction, and at whatever pace, suited their interests.

It was in this impasse that a body of intellectual Radicals
founded *The Westminster Review* in 1824. The travellers in the two
coaches were occupied with *The Edinburgh Review* and *The Quarterly*
which divided Ministerialists and anti-Ministerialists between
them. James Mill wrote a sensational article called 'The Edinburgh
Reviewed' for the first number, in which he blew the gaff on the
oligarchy in its two sections, their sham-fight and their two
periodicals. 'All that part of the aristocracy that think themselves
better off under the King's present advisers than they would be
otherwise, lend their influence to the Ministry. The opposition's

object is simply to change the hands that distribute the advantages of power. Apart from Court-intrigue, the great means of doing this is to operate upon the middling and lower classes. It did this by calling the aristocratic power despotic and popular demands anarchical, while itself operating a see-saw called 'the middle course, or moderation'. Looking back thirty-five years later when he wrote his celebrated *Autobiography*, John Mill described his father's article of 1824 as the most formidable attack on the Whig Party and policy ever made, and at the same time the greatest blow ever struck for English Radicalism. However that may be, no-one wishful to get below the surface of traditional party-politics could any longer be deceived into believing that the Reform Bill battles were to be understood, even at the political level, as contests between Whigs and Tories. There was in the field a mighty protagonist which bore no meaningful label, but which might—were the term admissable after the debasement of language in our century—be called 'the Third Force'. Those who led in party-politics knew it, even if they shrank from trying to name it or to describe it. It did not consist of those daring spirits who climbed to the top of the mound of Nottingham Castle to set fire to the Duke of Newcastle's house, or the men who set half Bristol ablaze, or even the citizens of London who marched back and forth roaring for 'The Bill, the whole Bill, and nothing less than the Bill!' so that young women trembled in their beds with terror. It had little to do with climbing, marching, torch-bearing. It had more to do with what an American President has called 'the silent majority'. Many of those who composed it may well have said with Mary Howitt, young wife of the Quaker apothecary who watched the Castle burning from the leads of the shop in Nottingham market-place: 'I who never in my life had been a politician, and where my prejudices from childhood had been in opposition to democracy, now most cordially allied myself with the party who cried out for radical reform'. For, as Mary wrote, 'the hopes of the poor were now centred on the Reform Bill . . . which it was believed would give them representation . . . ' Far from it. Many of them, like the majority of Orator Hunt's constituents at Preston, actually lost it. Like Peterloo itself, 1832 was the outward expression of a great upsurge of generous feeling.

CHAPTER 2

The Glories of King George IV

IT IS easily forgotten that Queen Victoria was by birth and early upbringing a Regency girl and that only the staid tutelage of the Prince Consort made her a Victorian. Albert found her frivolous to the point of exasperation, a young woman who loved nothing better than to dance all night and ride out at dawn to see the sun rise over London. Nor was her first Prime Minister, William Lamb, second Viscount Melbourne, likely to restrain her, himself being a black-browed Regency beauty of lounging manners and careless perfection of dress: no one, people said, ever *happened* to have coats that fitted better; an habitué of Carlton House and the Prince Regent. His tutelage of the young Queen preceded that of the Prince Consort, and she loved it, and him, 'Dear Lord M'.

Of all her Regency experiences, the one she always remembered best was being literally 'picked up' in the Park by her Uncle in his phaeton. Perched up beside the gorgeous mummy in mingled terror and delight all the way down to Virginia Water she replied to his gracious and civil questions as a young lady should who wishes to gain a memorable impression of her sovereign. He smelt of musk and macasser-oil, and he breathed like a grampus, puffing into a beautifully-flowered silk handkerchief and muttering: 'Dode gub too near, duck. God a fwightful code'. The Princess wouldn't have minded catching cold from a King, and when they came to Virginia Water and the Royal Band struck up loyal music, the King asked her what was her favourite tune, and she replied promptly: 'God save the King'. 'Good gurd, they shall blay it for you', her sovereign said, and they did.*

---

*Her choice has been said to be an early example of the tact for which she was afterwards famous. Lytton Strachey, however, thought it may well have been her real opinion, for, as he says, 'she was a very truthful child'.

Two things in later life reminded her of her Uncle Wales (they went on calling him that long after he ceased to be the P of W): one was the Gryphon in 'Alice', and the other was the Russian Bear in the cartoons of the Crimean War. Even the little that she had to do with him was an education in History, her favourite subject, for she never again imagined that her kinsmen who wore crowns and coronets were any less governed by their physical necessities than were coachmen and footmen, or needed to conceal the fact, which perhaps helps to explain why there were always jerries on hand in Victorian drawing-rooms, including Osborne and Windsor Castle. That, too, was why she laughed at the top of her voice when dear Sir Arthur Sullivan brought his Savoyards to Windsor to sing about being 'a right-down regular royal Queen'. For she had known all the time. They were very unkind about her poor Uncle Wales, but she always felt that she owed him a debt of gratitude for teaching her the human nature of the royal species to which she belonged.

And that, after all, was what mankind in general owed to George IV. As has been said of 'the last man in hell', someone had to be last, or lowest. George IV was both, and he may be said to have held a good many other 'all-time lows' as well. The best of it was that he seems to have known it. Every now and then he would begin to cry ('snivel' they said) because, as Victoria knew, he was really ashamed of himself. She knew also that he was right to be, but then so should a great many other people who weren't. Dear Uncle Wales, with his strong emotions and his strong smells, was at least as nice as her other Uncle, William, whom they called 'the old sea-dog', and who smelt of plug-tobacco and snuff and brandy. She always thought of him as another version of Jos Sedley in *Vanity Fair*. She never felt so tender to him because he was not so weak. And after all Uncle Wales had set on foot the reconstruction of Buckingham House as Buckingham Palace, the Queen's handsome, if not very cosy, London home.

It was in 1827, the year of Lord Liverpool's stroke, that there appeared a volume of engravings called *Metropolitan Improvements, or London in the 19th Century*, which put on record the new buildings of George IV's London. No other King of England is associated with a tithe of the splendours associated with the name of

George IV. He changed England from a country of rural resi-
dences and *cottages ornées* to a land of urban amenities. Before, it
was not too much to say that the best English architecture was
strictly rural. England had towns, but they were hardly more than
clusters of village-streets dominated by the Gothic towers or
spires of ancient and beautiful parish churches. Nowhere did one
come upon the real *urbs* except occasionally where the ground had
been cleared by the accident of fire, as at Blandford Forum, or
where modern man had established a spa, as at Bath, or Chelten-
ham, or Tunbridge Wells, or (in a half-hearted way) Buxton, or
Leamington. As city-builders or town-dwellers the English were
as ignominious as rabbits. It was George IV who changed all that,
mostly when he was still Regent. The pity was that he did not
come to the throne ten years before he did. 'I am too old to build
a Palace', he said when he set about remodelling Buckingham
House. All the same he did not do at all badly. Whether or not he
was present at the battle of Waterloo, as he liked to make out, no
one has ever given a victorious people a more magnificent gift of
celebration than King George IV gave a people who rather natur-
ally grumbled about his extravagance and deplored his immorality.
A lot of his work was to be messed about in the generations of
plutocracy and even more by the democracy that followed, but
London has never since ceased to be altogether facially recog-
nizable as a capital city.

George IV was consciously out-bidding Paris in architectural
glories. He could not see why the victorious people should be
inferior to the defeated in any branch of achievement. In 1812
even before the downfall of Napoleon, and even before he was
King, he laid a sword upon the shoulders of the Cornish hero of
the safety-lamp, Humphrey Davy. Davy's career had been the
scientific romance of the Regency, and now proceeded to make
the reign of George IV as glorious for science as for architecture.
A number of men claimed to have invented the miner's safety-
lamp, including George Stephenson, of whom Davy said cattily
that it was true he had invented a safety-lamp but it was not safe,
an observation that was perhaps forgivable when it came from a
man whose scientific achievements were so many and varied as
those of Humphrey Davy. He had beaten the distinguished

Frenchman, Guy-Lussac, in establishing the basic chemistry of
iodine while on a visit to the enemy capital in 1815, working with
his portable apparatus in a hotel-bedroom. When he became Professor of Chemistry at the London Institution they had to install
private boxes in the lecture-theatre in Albemarle Street in order to
cope with fashionable London's crowded attendance at the magician's demonstrations, a popular phenomenon which had been in-
augurated by Davy's dispensation of 'the laughing-gas', or pure
nitrous oxide from a silken bag at next-to-nothing a sniff. There
came a point when Sir Joseph Banks, first chairman of the
managers of the Institution, withdrew with the remark that it was
'now entirely in the hands of the prophane'. Davy was hardly
responsible for the fact that chemistry, always a dramatic form of
science, was now at the stage when such elementary effects as
explosion, effervescence and bright lights drew crowds of specta-
tors. Behind and beyond these dramatic features, however, people
were beginning to realise that science was to be a mighty factor in
the future of civilisation. Scientific discovery in England had
always gone hand in hand with technical achievement, and Davy
himself never missed an opportunity to stress the 'utility' of
science. His Inaugural Lecture as Professor of Chemistry was an
exordium on the beneficent alliance of men of science and manufacturers, the bright prospects ahead for the enlightenment and
happiness of a humanity united by means of knowledge and the
useful arts. 'We do not look to distant ages', he said, 'We look for
a time that we may reasonably expect—FOR A BRIGHT DAY
OF WHICH WE ALREADY BEHOLD THE DAWN.'

Davy's career, from Cornish fisher-boy to his country's most
distinguished man of science, redeems the reign of George IV,
like the terraces of Regent's Park. It was the last time that a man
could be both a working scientist and a poet. His friend S. T.
Coleridge, who was a fine judge of such things, once said of
Humphrey Davy that if he had not been the first chemist he would
have been the first poet of his age. He wrote science, and delivered
lectures on science, like a poet, and a Romantic Poet at that,
erasing errors by drawing his inky finger across the page. Like
most Romantics who turn to science, he could never resist the
role of the alchemist, even the magician. When he decomposed

and recomposed the fixed alkalis by electrolysis, when he decomposed water at a touch, when he named the new metals he had isolated 'Potassium' and 'Sodium', he seemed to resemble the Almighty Himself who alone was the giver of names to the creatures of His creation. The jest was to be put about that he 'lived in the odium of having discovered sodium'. Unfortunately for the jesters, they could find no rhyme for Davy apart from 'gravy', a dietary constituent of which he was very fond. He lived for a little less than ten years under George IV, dying at the early age of fifty-one among the Italians who affectionately called him 'Siromfredevi'. Before he died he completed his book *Consolations in Travel, or the Last Days of a Philosopher*, which consists of a Vision and six Dialogues vouched unto the Philosopher in the Colosseum in Rome. Davy, an exemplar of so many features of modern science, appears to have invented Well's Time-machine, which enables him to give a kind of running-commentary on the panorama of history. In doing so, he reveals a typical nineteenth-century contempt for the environment of 'The Noble Savage', and an Arnoldian reverence for the ages of Greece and Rome. His attitude to the Goths is a nice mixture of Gibbon and Charles Kingsley. While destroying Roman power, they were yet the instrument of divine power which gave energy to a debilitated population. With the Renaissance and the Reformation, society took on its modern and permanent aspect. Printing made the productions of human genius imperishable, and by the invention of gunpowder wars became less bloody and less personal. Speaking in the reign of George IV Davy's 'Genius' could confidently assert that gunpowder gave permanence to the triumphs of the human mind and secured the cultivated nations from ever again being over-run by barbarians. He takes no account of the possibility of the barbarians coming from within, and his story of the progress of mankind ends in true Victorian style with the vision of one nation 'pre-eminent for her maritime strength, and colonial and commercial enterprise', a nation which 'retains her superiority only because it is favourable to the liberty of mankind'.

It was at this point that Sir Humphrey Davy became, as one always suspected that he might, a pioneer of space-fiction. The Genius, or Time-traveller, whom he calls the Genius, promptly lifts Siromfredevi right out of the cold dim cavern of the Colosseum into the bright and luminous regions of inter-stellar space. Enclosed in what he calls 'a moving sphere of light' he passes by the moon and stars 'as if it were in my power to touch them with my hand', until he stood upon the verge of the solar system and gazed upon the double ring of Saturn. The purpose of this trans lunar journey was soon apparent. He was going to Heaven, or rather to visit a whole series of Heavens, the dwelling places of spiritual and intellectual natures as superior to man as man is superior to the common house-fly. In fact in this, his journey through space, Davy enacts the last Act of Shaw's *Back to Methuselah* a hundred years before Shaw. In these cold bright planetary spaces he has travelled 'as far as thought can reach', and the beings he meets there comprise a scale of intellectual being which makes the evolution of man from the protoplasm to Plato look like the first rather dingy inch of a measuring rod extending from Charing Cross to the Seventh Heaven. The lowest grade of these higher natures 'moved from place to place by six extremely thin membranes, which they used as wings', and the upper parts of their bodies were composed of 'numerous convolutions of tubes, more analagous to the trunk of the elephant . . . ' They possessed, as the Genius explained, 'a sphere of sensibility and intellectual enjoyment far superior to that of the inhabitants of your earth . . . Their sources of pleasure are of the highest intellectual nature . . . their minds are in unceasing activity, and this activity is a source of perpetual enjoyment . . . the objects of their ambition are entirely those of intellectual greatness . . . '

About each of the planets, from Saturn to the sun, there moved 'peculiar intellectual beings bearing analogies to each other, and yet all different in power and essence', the highest of all being a species of seraph. 'The universe is everywhere full of life', declares the Genius, 'but the modes of this life are infinitely diversified, and yet every form of it must be enjoyed and known by every spiritual nature before the consumation of all things . . . The spiritual natures pass from system to system in progression towards power and knowledge.' If the passion for power and knowledge is misapplied or abused at any stage in the process, 'the being is degraded, it sinks in the scale of existence, and still belongs to the earth or an inferior system, till its errors are corrected by painful discipline.' The highest experience of all is to 'feel the personal presence of that supreme Deity which you only imagine; to you belongs faith, to us knowledge; and our greatest delight results from the conviction that we are lights kindled at his light, and that we belong to his substance . . . we know all things begin from and end in his everlasting presence, the cause of causes, the power of powers . . . '

Davy's vision in the Colosseum amounts to the spiritual testament of a creative evolutionist. Like the Victorians, however, he could not leave it at that. The Vision has to be discussed in a series of dialogues between a liberal Catholic, a sceptic, and a mysterious person called 'The Unknown',—evidently Davy's *alter ego*, a philosophic pilgrim who is discovered seated on a camp-stool among the ruins of Paestum 'writing in a memorandum-book', and wearing around his neck a phial containing chlorine. This substitution of chlorine for the crucifix, or the combination of chemistry and Christianity, may serve as a rather crude symbol of the intellectual position of Davy himself, who had demonstrated the nature of chlorine in one of his most brilliant papers for the Royal Society, in 1810, thereafter carrying it with him on his wanderings among the marshes of southern Italy as a preventive against malarial fever. 'The Unknown' is a religiose scientist, or a scientific religionist, a truly typical figure of nineteenth-century philosophy who steers the Dialogues to a suitably modernist but Christian conclusion.

Humphrey Davy's position in the history of science possesses a significance far beyond the realm of physical discovery. He was a portent in the history of the general mind of his race and his age. The fact that he felt himself concerned to relate his scientific work to the great questions of philosophy is in itself a historical fact of the first magnitude. The fact that he failed to accomplish it effectively is scarcely less momentous. In a world where science and philosophy (more especially the philosophy of religion) were turning their backs on each other, he attempted—perhaps he was the last to attempt—to bring about not only a reconciliation but a synthesis. The fact that he failed may in part be ascribed to his own philosophical short-comings. In the main, however, it was due to the gigantic proportions which such a task had assumed by his time. The measure of his unsuccess is the measure of the extent to which the fragmentation of human knowledge had already made inevitable the division of labour in the world of modern thought. He was the last man of science to write like a poet and to wear the name of 'philosopher' with the pride of lineage. 'Natural, and moral, and religious knowledge are of one family', he observed, 'and happy is that country, and great is its strength, where they dwell together in union'.

CHAPTER 3

The Coming of Reform

MANY MEN have died of attending other men's funerals. This was perhaps what Thomas Pelham, Duke of Newcastle, was thinking about when he planted himself on the long train of the Duke of Cumberland to keep his feet from the sepulchral chill of the Abbey floor at the burial of George II. Cumberland, lame and paralytic, died soon of the cold that should have killed Newcastle. Much the same thing happened to George Canning when, having induced the old Earl of Eldon to stand on his hat, he took to his bed of a chill from which he never recovered. This time the tragedy was the greater because it critically changed the course of history. Canning was only fifty-seven, and after the long dispensation of Lord Liverpool the country needed a leader of Canning's political genius. Instead she was given the Duke of Wellington, of whom Coleridge once observed that he was too much disposed to imagine that he could govern a great nation by word of command in the same way in which he governed a highly disciplined army. The old warrior (he was only a year older than Canning, but having lived so great and glorious a life in half a century, he always seemed an *old* soldier) had made up his mind about everything many years ago, and what England needed was a man with a flexible mind in order to cope with the problems of the post-war age. Canning had that, and now he was dead before he could meet the House of Commons as Prime Minister.

Men of all shades of opinion had looked to him. He was the hope of 'those stern unbending Tories' as certainly as he was the toast of young men whose minds and imaginations dwelt on new things in a new world. The hopes that were placed in George Canning were manifold and various. To many he was simply the latterday disciple of the great Mr Pitt. To many more he was the political man of the future. Henry Lytton Bulwer included him in the Second Volume of his *Historical Characters* as the personification of 'The Brilliant Man'. With the death of his old rival, not to say enemy, Castlereagh, he had arrived at the Foreign Office where his talents found most scope and his career was marked by the great achievements in the cause of national self-determination in the Old World and the New for which he will always be remembered. Castlereagh had initiated the country's departure from the Holy Alliance with which his name was for long unjustly associated. Canning boldly withdrew England from the Congress System and set her unequivocally on the side of European liberties and national independence. He was indeed in most respects the first major English statesman to earn, and deserve, the name of Liberal. Like his chief, Lord Liverpool, he was a Liberal Tory, although he was firmly opposed to parliamentary reform. When at the departure of Liverpool he was entrusted by George IV with the task of forming an administration, seven of Liverpool's Ministerial colleagues refused to serve under him, partly because of his intention to espouse the cause of Catholic Emancipation, and partly out of personal dislike, for Canning had the misfortune to be a wit and had made enemies with his tongue. At the same time a number of liberally-minded Whigs were willing to support him, although Earl Grey never forgot or forgave his attacks upon him in *The Anti-Jacobin*. Grey, like Canning during the years of his hostility for Castlereagh, was biding his time, and Canning's death in 1827 removed the old enemy of Anti-Jacobin days. The long-lived feud between the two men, who were the choicest parliamentary spirits of their day, was perhaps the last legacy of the old embitterment surviving from the days when the French Revolution had breached so many old friendships. After all, Grey had started his political career as an ardent Foxite. The Fox-Burke estrangement was repeated in the estrangement of Grey and Canning.

When Wellington took over within twelve months of Canning's death, he stood firm against Parliamentary Reform but he brought in the measure of Catholic Emancipation which the great Liberal-Tory had for so long advocated. He soon lost the support of the Canningites who, unlike their master, now advocated the reform of parliament. In the later months of 1830 the Duke's supporters had shrunk so far that he was compelled to resign, and, when the King called upon Earl Grey and the Whigs, the Canningites of course went in with him. Thus the conjunction of Grey and Canning was achieved after Canning's death in a manner of speaking. By this time with an Administration composed of Whigs and Canningites, under the Premiership of a man who had been associated with every attempt at Parliamentary Reform for the last forty years and with three future Prime Ministers in its ranks, it seemed to the friends of Reform that victory could not be far away. Even so, Grey's first Parliamentary Reform Bill passed the Commons by a majority of only one vote. When Grey brought in a Second Bill after a General Election later in the year it was rejected by the Lords. It was the Third Bill introduced in December, 1831, that passed both Houses in the summer of 1832. The high feeling, the clamour, even the threat of civil war which accompanied the final campaign belong to the autumn and winter of 1831–32. What Grey querulously called 'constant and active pressure from without' was crucial. This pressure was the culmination of activity 'out-of-doors' since the end of the War, the theme of my previous volume, *Waterloo to Peterloo*, and it makes sense of the view that the Great Reform Bill was the will of 'the people', finally brought about by them. If it is to be understood it requires to be seen in a much greater historical perspective than that afforded by parliamentary history or the contest of the two coaches of Hazlitt.*

No one could have been better adapted to preside over this crisis than William IV, who succeeded to his brother, George IV, in 1830. In politics 'The Sailor King' was in most respects the nautical equivalent of the Duke of Wellington, that is to say the mainspring of his character and conduct was an unswerving devotion to duty. As Wellington used to say: 'I am *nimmukwallah*, as we say in the East; that is, I have ate of the King's salt, and, therefore, I conceive it to be my duty to serve with unhesitating zeal and cheerfulness, when and wherever the King or his government may think proper to employ me'. William IV, when Duke of Clarence, had served in the Navy where he came under the spell

*See Chapter 1, p. 6.

of Nelson, whom he continued to love to the end of his days. *Nimmukwallah*, as used of a King, could only mean—or could mean no less than—devotion to *kingly* duty. When it became at length apparent that it was his duty to overcome the resistance of the House of Lords to the Reform Bill, he put aside his intense dislike of promising to create new Peers for such a purpose. His action was the counterpart of the Duke of Wellington's act of supreme statesmanship at the same moment when, as it has been said, 'he drew in his long legs and let the Bill pass'. He had fought to the last ditch, but there he stopped, on the ground presumably that 'the King's government must be carried on'. It would have been absurd for William IV to have made a remark like that, but that is what he meant. There comes a point in every lost battle where resistance is the course of neither a soldier nor statesman.

The activities which brought about the passing of the Great Reform Bill were only at the surface of political and parliamentary life those of Grey and Russell who drafted the legislation in Down-ing Street and passed it at Westminster and whose story has been told *ad nauseam*. Thirty-five years ago Simon Maccoby protested in the Preface of his *English Radicalism 1832–1852* against this restricted version of the history of the early nineteenth century. One of the first-fruits of that protest was the work preceding the present volume, which attempted to restore a wider perspective to the years between Waterloo and Peterloo. To carry the story on from Peterloo to the opening of the Victorian Age is an altogether simpler task, for once the Great Reform Bill was on the Statute Book as an Act of Parliament we are suddenly in another world. As Sir James Butler has put it, 'we leave the remote world of the eighteenth century, peopled by the heroic ghosts of Pitt and Fox and Canning, for the era of Peel and Palmerston, of the Corn Laws and the Crimea. The old aristocratic system begins to crumble, and the feet of the nation are set in the path that leads to demo-cracy.'

William IV was ideally suited to the task of leading the nation onward in that direction, for he had few hereditary prejudices, save that like most Kings he was a Conservative. Like his contem-porary, Louis Philippe, King of the French, ('The Umbrella King') he liked going for walks in his capital in plain clothes. His father,

George III, had always liked going about as a plain country-gentleman, popping into the fishmonger's to ask the price of cod. This was, however, when he wanted to take soundings about the chances of his favourite candidates at election-times. The good old King was always a trifle eccentric. His son William's eccentricities were rather those of an old sailor, the best-known being the snotty, or midshipman, habit of wiping his nose on the back of his forefinger. It was perhaps a trifle worrying for his entourage, in an age without plain-clothes detectives, for the King to wander off among hackney-coach men and porters, chatting amiably to Tom, Dick and Harry. He was always liked if seldom venerated or admired, a paradigm of the common man before the category was invented.

He was past his sixty-fourth birthday when they brought him the news early on a summer morning in 1830 that his brother was dead and that he was now King of England. It is said that he announced his intention of staying in bed a little longer because he had never been in bed with a queen before and wished to make the most of it. If Charles II had said it, this observation would have been quoted forever after as a prime example of royal wit, but as William IV said it—or so it was rumoured—it was to remain simply as an example of royal buffoonery. His people got used to their sovereign saying such things. At the end of dinner, it was reported that he would push back his chair and announce: 'Now ladies and gentlemen, we will disperse to our several amusements. I am going to bed with the Queen, and I hope you will enjoy yourselves, too.' People reminded themselves that His Majesty had served in the Navy, and 'you know what sailors are'. His indiscretions were blunt, honest, outspoken, untroubled by considerations of taste, redolent of his habitual attachment to truth. As the horse-dealer assures his customers, he was 'without vice', which certainly made a change after George IV. To serve an habitually truthful King saved a great deal of trouble. Pig-headed and liable to fuss about little things, he left no room for ambiguity in matters great or small.

He had been King for scarcely twelve months when the crisis over the Reform Bill broke. There had been a Revolution in Paris in the previous year, and the King, Charles X, had had to leave in something of a hurry. This is said to have encouraged the reform movement in London, although many of the election contests that year were over by the time that the news of the July Revolution reached England. There is no reason to suppose that William IV needed to be admonished by the example of events in Paris as to the fate of reactionary monarchs. His refusal to create enough new Peers to afford the Reform Bill a sufficient majority in the House of Lords was no doubt maddening for the Ministers, but it was like most other things about his conduct at all times entirely honourable. As Coleridge said, the Ministers had been guilty of two things pre-eminently wicked in their conduct of the Bill: they had played upon the passions and ignorance of the nation, but worse than that they had made the King the prime mover in political wickedness, making him tell his people that they had been deprived of their rights, indeed had been enslaved for a century past, thereby vilifying the memory of his own brother and his father. Whether or not these considerations were at the root of William's objection to creating Peers, he gave way when it became apparent that the people would have the Bill. At this point Coleridge said that he had heard but two arguments in favour of passing it: (1) We will blow your brains out if you don't pass it; (2) We will drag you through a horse-pond if you don't pass it. There was, he thought, a good deal of force in both . . . The one thing you could feel quite certain about of William IV was his patriotism. He seemed, as his brother George once said, to have run away with all his family's stock of good sense.

The reigns of kings and queens have a way of mattering a good deal more than pert young historians will admit in an age that likes to imagine itself to have outlived monarchy. Not, of course, as chronological landmarks, although even there they have their uses. It is only in the case of long reigns that they have much use as stylistic labels. Everyone knows what is meant by 'Elizabethan' or 'Victorian', while 'Caroline' and 'Jacobean' continue to ring bells. But whoever thought of talking about 'Wilhelmine'? Of the three former Williams, the first was the Norman Conqueror, the second was 'Rufus', and the third was 'the Protestant hero' or 'Our Great Restorer'. The fourth lacked all semblance of heroic proportions. He has enjoyed only the distinction of appearing on inn-

B

signboards in the rolled collar and snowy wig of an admiral, a telescope under his arm and a buckled shoe on a fourteen-pound cannon. Our last Hanoverian prince had the bluff features of an English sea-dog. A better fate perhaps than to be commemorated as Adonis or Florizel or the First Gentleman. There is even a faint likelihood that he did something to salvage the Monarchy, for when Victoria took it up after his death it quickly became a success, almost as if there had been a hiatus since the death of her grandfather, 'the Good Old King'. Like George III, Victoria reigned for fifty years. In his seven, William IV achieved much in making it possible to forget George IV.

CHAPTER 4

The Feast of the Barmecide*

As AN act of state, the measure of reform enacted in 1832 of course took the form of a parliamentary statute, so that it could be said with superficial truth that it was the unreformed House of Commons that reformed the unreformed House of Commons. Many men who defended the old order—incidentally earning for themselves lasting ridicule—did so on precisely the ground that it was a self-adjusting institution. And for a number of years it had been doing just that. S. T. Coleridge, that shrewd observer of how things happen as distinct from how they happen in books, when he wrote his *Constitution of the Church and State* in 1829, urged would-be reformers to consider carefully whether a great deal had not already been done by social and economic changes in the community: 'roads, canals, machinery, the periodical and daily press, the might of public opinion, the consequent increasing desire of popularity among public men and functionaries of every description, the increasing necessity of public character as a means or condition of political influence. I need but mention these to stand acquitted of having started a vague and naked possibility in extenuation of an evident and palpable abuse.' Certain unrepresented places and interests actually availed themselves of the defects of the imperfect representative system in order to secure the services of Members without constituents, 'retaining' them, so to speak, by means of what was in fact an abuse. The system—should—as Coleridge said—have provided for a periodic 'revisal and re-adjustment'. No one in his senses would cite this state of affairs as evidence of the meritorious nature of the unreformed system, although it might serve in its extenuation. So, too, might

*Name of Arabian-nights Prince whose feast to a beggar was rich dish-covers with nothing beneath them.

the well-known fact that the old House enabled men who were physically unfitted for the rough and tumble of a populous constituency to serve the nation in Parliament. Even after 1832 this fact was illustrated by the case of Robert Lowe, an albino and almost blind, who sat for Lord Lansdowne's pocket-borough of Calne. Bright young men, too, could enter the House of Commons while their brains were yet unaddled by the routine of electioneering, although it is true that a host of nonentities owed their parliamentary presence to the same avenue. A man who had entered the House for a 'close-borough' seems to have taken the first opportunity to exchanging it for an open one.

The House of Commons which was the scene of these antics was not so much a workshop of legislation as a clearing-house for the property-deals of the aristocracy. Much the greater part of the House's legislative work was concerned with private bills, enclosure acts, canal acts, turnpike-trust acts. If it were to become a legislative workshop it would have to be radically changed. One of the most cogent reasons for change was to remove from the House some of the mistrust which intelligent men felt for it as an agent of social reformation. As Thomas Carlyle said in his chapters on 'Laissez-faire' and 'Not Laissez-faire' in *Chartism* (1839), what people really meant when they asked to be left alone was not that they thought that human affairs needed no guidance, but 'Leave us alone of *your* guidance', for 'such guidance is worse than none!' John Stuart Mill said much the same. 'The *let alone* doctrine, or the theory that governments can do no better than to do nothing', he said was 'generated by the manifest selfishness and incompetence of modern European governments . . . ' The State, it had been found, was a bad judge of the wants of society, indeed cared little for them, and when it attempted anything beyond a minimal attention to crime and the few things indispensable to mere social existence it was generally moved only by the 'private sinister interest' of a class. It might be expected that a more fairly elected House of Commons would be more trustworthy. 1832 was the first step in that direction.

'Having got parliamentary reform . . . ', said Cobbett, 'my resentment was becoming blunted. But the Poor Law Bill I could not stomach!' Nor could most other champions of the poor.

Everyone but the Whigs and the political-economists denounced it as an invasion of the property of the poor. By curtailing 'outdoor relief' the New Poor Law was robbing the poor of the compensation which had been given them in compensation for the monastic charity taken from them at the Dissolution of the Monasteries. Thus argued also the young Benjamin D'Israeli, and thus argued all who spoke of the New Poor Law as an invasion of the civil rights of the English people. The People's Charter and the New Poor Law could be ascribed to the same origin. Cobbett insisted that amongst the rights we all inherited from our forefathers was the right to have a living out of the land of our birth, and, if we fell into distress, to have our wants relieved out of the produce of the land. The Poor rates were compensation for what had been taken away when the aristocracy stole monastic charities and tithes, both of which had been mainly intended for the relief of the poor and distressed. The taking away of those rates by the New Poor Law was as much an invasion of rights as would be the withholding of the landlord's rents. Popular hatred of the new Poor Law was the loudest and fiercest element in the Chartist agitation.

And yet, as Carlyle said, 'Nature makes nothing in vain; not even a Poor Law Amendment Act'. He went on to welcome it as 'the harsh beginning of much, the harsh ending of much'. For there was no doubt, could be no doubt, that the refusal of outdoor relief was, as he said, 'the one thing needful'. The Poor Law and its associated Speenhamland policy, was 'a bounty of unthrift, idleness, bastardy and beer-drinking . . . ' The law of 'No work, no recompense' needed to be enforced, and not only on the manual worker. 'We will praise the New Poor Law, farther, as the probable preliminary of some general charge to be taken of the lowest classes by the higher.' But what the champions of the New Poor Law were really interested in was the reduction of the rates in order to lessen the burden on agriculture, amounting to more than 8 million a year as compared with 5 or at the most 6 million, at the opening of the century. Nor was the relief of the agricultural ratepayer necessarily a selfish or merely sectional benefit in what was still a predominantly agricultural community.

Two years after the Poor Law Amendment Act, Parliament

passed the Municipal Corporations Act of 1835, which put the government of corporate towns into the hands of elected councils on a franchise a great deal wider than that instituted by the Act of 1832 for election of Members of Parliament, that is to say, all who paid poor and borough rates. It had been said at the time of Peterloo, that if Manchester had been a corporate town, and certainly if it had been governed by its own citizens, that tragedy would never have happened, for it had been essentially a blunder committed by a rural magistracy intruded into a town they hardly knew. The Municipal Corporations Act of 1835 set up a framework of local government which was to transform English towns from overgrown villages into effective and efficient urban communities. Here rather than in the much-lauded Great Reform Bill was the real beginning of modern government in England. Here, too, was a reform measure that could bring about radical changes in English society without calling down curses upon its promoters, for it had none of the grim and dramatic features which were to be memorialised (wrongly) in *Oliver Twist*. The least dramatic, it was also the least 'Barmecidal' of the legislative fruits of Reform.

The somewhat fruitless character of the search for beneficent legislation consequent upon the passing of the Great Reform Bill need surprise no one who has grasped the extent of the reforms instituted before that measure. Perhaps it is the human liking for dramatic Denouncements, more especially in school-textbooks, permitting the introduction of sub-headings like 'Triumph of Democracy' or 'Downfall of Despotism' in capital letters, terms that arouse unjustifiable expectations and prohibit slow transitions. It is easy to assume that 'reforms' before 1832 were not only unlikely to occur but if they did occur were unlikely to be reforms. A brief list of measures that did arrive in those years, more especially in the years 1823–1829, shows that this is nothing more than an assumption, and an ill-grounded one. Immediately with the replacement of Sidmouth by Peel as Home Secretary there commenced that reform of the Criminal Law which was greatly to reduce the number of capital offences, and in the following year the Combination Acts which had prohibited the formation of Trade Unions for so long were modified. This last has often been described as the 'repeal' of the Combination Laws, although the modified re-imposition of the laws followed in the year 1825 after an outbreak of industrial strikes when the Prime Minister made his celebrated confession to the House of Commons that he had not properly understood what the 'repeal' amounted to. Perhaps more important was Peel's institution of the Metropolitan Police force in 1829. Few things have ever done more to promote law and order without bitterness than the recruitment of an unarmed non-political police-force on a local basis. The 'Bobbies' or 'Peelers' were to remain the best-known eponymous institution of nineteenth century England. The government of industrial England by soldiers and spies had come to an end within less than ten years. 'From Peterloo to the Peelers' might stand as the title of an epoch.

Two acts of the first Reformed Parliament in 1833 tackled slavery at home and abroad. The Slave Trade, the abominable traffic in Negroes, had been abolished by law in 1807 after many years of humanitarian endeavour. In 1833 the slaves were emancipated in the British Empire, their owners receiving twenty million pounds in compensation. That same year, largely as a result of the endeavours of Lord Shaftesbury, the hours of labour of women and children in factories was effectively restricted by statute. A good deal was said at the time, and has been said since, about 'white slavery' in this country, Caddy Jellaby and her like. That year also saw Parliament granting money for the first time for the elementary education of the nation's children. The sum of £20,000 not 20 million, was voted for this purpose. The two voluntary societies which had devoted themselves to the task, the National Society, and the British and Foreign Schools Society, had been building and maintaining schools for the children of the poor since their foundation twenty years before. They based their teaching on the maxim 'what a boy can learn, a boy can teach', or the Monitorial Method, which enabled large numbers of pupils to be instructed cheaply. The monitorial schools were in fact the factory system applied to education. They were, as one of their advocates said, 'comparable to the most ingenious inventions in the mechanical department'. Coleridge himself spoke of the method as 'an especial gift of Providence to the human race . . . this incomparable machine, this vast moral steam-engine' although he warned against supposing that it, of itself, formed an efficient national education. The danger was that people might imagine themselves to have solved the problem of mass-education on a minimum of expenditure. It certainly postponed for many years the proper training of teachers.

It had been coming for a long time, the education-mania. 'L'éducation peut tout', the French had said in the days of La Chalotais, and there was an 'education-mad party' here by the eighteen-twenties. As Winthrop Mackworth Praed wrote:

> The schoolmaster's abroad you see,
> And when the people hear him speak
> They all insist on being free,
> And reading Homer in the Greek . . .

Coleridge, when he wrote his first Lay Sermon in 1817, said that 'the powers that awaken and foster the spirit of curiosity are to be found in every village; books are in every hovel'. And, in case anyone wished to complain of the inconveniences that had arisen from education having become too general, he would recommend their removal by making it universal.

Cheap and plentiful books was the obvious answer, and the pioneer of the 'paperback-revolution' of the 1820's was Henry Brougham, the Scottish advocate with a long nose, a pert manner, and enormous ambition. No one trusted him for very long, and he never rose to political altitudes aside from the Woolsack. He was prepared to speak and write on anything, a sort of Encyclopedia in breeches. Someone said of him that if Brougham knew a little law he would know something of everything. This smatterer was a sincere champion of popular education, the leading figure of the 'education-mad party'. He was the founder of the Society for the Diffusion of Useful Knowledge, the 'Learned Friend' of Peacock's novel, *Crochet Castle,* where he figures as the head of the 'Steam-Intellect Society'. He published scores of little books for the Society, mostly on popular science, at sixpence a volume. There was also his Library of Entertaining Knowledge, equally cheap, and (what bankrupted the Society in the end) 'The Penny Cyclopedia'. All this popular pabulum was put forth for the members of Brougham's protégé, the Mechanics' Institute. Bentham used to address Brougham, in whom he had great faith as a law-reformer, as 'Dear Poppet', and the man was a god-send to the caricaturists, with his long proboscis, which bore no resemblance to a beak, and his jovial air of mild debauchery. He bore a close resemblance to W. S. Gilbert's 'susceptible Chancellor' in *Iolanthe,* and still more to the judge in *Trial by Jury,* who told the Jury: 'Put your briefs upon the shelf, I will marry her myself'. He had led for the defence of Queen Caroline on the charge of adultery, and, like a large number of public men who took her side, was said to have gone to bed with her.

So, one by one, between Peterloo and the Victorian Age, the familiar features of a modern society were being evolved: Penguin Books (under another name), the poor-law, the police-force, the elementary school: the typical institutions of the modern industrial state. When they were deplored by Robert Southey in his *Colloquies on the Progress and Prospects of Society* in 1829 and contrasted very much to their demerit with the features of the older society known to Sir Thomas More (who takes an important part in the book), Southey was taken severely to task by Macaulay as an intellectual Luddite. 'Here is wisdom', exclaimed the brilliant young reviewer in the *Edinburgh.* 'Here are the principles on which nations are to be governed. Rose-bushes and poor-rates, rather than steam-engines and independence . . . Mr Southey has found out a way he tells us, in which the effects of manufacturers and agriculture may be compared. And what is this way? To stand on a hill, to look at a cottage and a factory, and to see which is the prettier.' And it was true that Southey had let himself go about the sheer ugliness of industrial society. 'How is it', the old Luddite* had asked, 'that everything which is connected with manufactures presents such features of unqualified deformity?' It was another, and infinitely greater poet, from the country of the Luddites, who declared that 'though perhaps nobody knew it, it was ugliness which really betrayed the spirit of man in the nineteenth century'. D. H. Lawrence was writing almost exactly a hundred years later.

*Spiritually of course. The notion of his taking to the sledge-hammer is ludicrous.

CHAPTER 5

The Poverty of Poetry

It was, as might perhaps be expected, a bad time for poetry, as if Peterloo had made the English air unfit for poets to breathe. The abhorred shears certainly went to work with peculiar zest upon the young in the years between the 'massacre' and the Bill. While the young men died, old Scott, and Southey, and Mrs Hemans went on living into the 'thirties. The Ancient Mariner, or 'the grey-headed passenger' as he was now calling himself, still lived up at Highgate, talking like an angel, though most people had no very clear notion what about. Thomas de Quincey was writing his impassioned prose, and William Wordsworth was still writing poetry which too often seemed like unimpassioned prose. Samuel Rogers and John Keble poetised, while Leigh Hunt and Bulwer Lytton prosed. When the new luminaries of the Victorian Age arose, they seemed to rise into an empty sky, all appearing above the horizon at once. By the 1850's it was said that you met immortals in every street. In the twenties and thirties there had been a strange vacancy, as if the world were waiting for the rebirth of genius, the dawn of an age more propitious to their kind of activity.

The gods, it seemed, were angry, bent on dashing the dawn in darkness. Morning had been heralded by the greatest harbingers ever to cry the dawn of a new age of poetry. 'Great spirits now on earth are sojourning', Keats said in 1817, and he spoke not only of Wordsworth and the older men but of 'other spirits . . . standing apart upon the forehead of the age to come' who would 'give the world another heart, and other pulses'. For he thought he heard 'the hum of mighty workings . . . ' Shelley, too, had spoken at almost the same time of a new birth of literature which was, he thought, 'the most unfailing herald' of national revival. He felt

himself to be living among 'such philosophers and poets as sur-
pass beyond comparison any who have appeared in our nation
since the last struggle for liberty', by which presumably he meant
the seventeenth century. A few months before Shelley wrote these
words in his unpublished *Philosophical View of Reform* his friend
Thomas Love Peacock had composed his paradoxical essay, *The
Four Ages of Poetry*, in which his own time was identified with the
fourth and latest, the Age of Brass. No doubt Peacock's essay was
a *jeu d'esprit*, remembered now only because it brought forth
Shelley's great essay, *In Defence of Poetry,* which concludes with
some of the most sublime claims that were ever made for the poet.
In this essay the poet becomes 'a nightingale who sits in darkness
and sings to cheer its own solitude with sweet sounds', not to mention the hierophant of an unapprehended inspiration, the mirror
of the gigantic shadows which futurity casts upon the present, and
(best known of all) the unacknowledged legislator of the world.
Peacock, a child of the eighteenth century, a wit, a sceptic, much
as he loved Shelley (the Scythrop of *Nightmare Abbey*) could hardly
be expected to take this. A poet in modern times, he would tell us,
is 'a semi-barbarian in a civilized community', and poetry is only
cultivated to the neglect of some more useful branch of study,
something outgrown with the childhood of the race. As the
youthful Macaulay was to say a few years later in his first brilliant
essay for the *Edinburgh* (*Milton*, 1825), 'perhaps no person can be a
poet, or can enjoy poetry, without a certain unsoundness of mind'.
That kind of remark was not at all rare in the mouths of respectable and responsible, as well as 'brilliant' men at that time. Poetry
was 'a mere jingle that proves no facts', said Professor John
Millar, lecturing on Law in the University of Glasgow. After all
the world was noisy with steam-engines and the scholastic adum-
brations of Thomas Gradgrind, and it was only a few years since
Jeremy Bentham announced that 'all poetry is misrepresentation'.

It was that arid civil servant, Sir Henry Taylor, who produced
the manifesto of the movement, a loud bassoon after Peacock's tin
whistle. In his preface to his poetic-drama *Philip van Artevelde* in
1834, he admonished poets to stop turning out luxuries and to
walk the common earth and breathe the common air. 'I would by
no means wish to be understood as saying that a poet can be too

imaginative', he was careful to say, 'provided that his other faculties be exercised in due proportion to his imagination . . . I would have no man depress his imagination, but I would have him raise his reason to be its equipoise.' What Sir Henry wished to oppugn was 'the strange notion which seems to prevail amongst certain of our writers and readers of poetry that good sense stands in a position of antagonism to practical genius, instead of being one of its most essential constituents. Unless the two are combined we get rhapsody, melody, visionariness, but not poetry in its highest sense. Poetry is Reason's sense sublimed . . . ' Like Peacock, he professes to discern such defects especially in the poets of the Age of Brass who cultivated 'the return to nature'. Instead of keeping pace with the historian and the philosopher in their concern for the advance of learning they deliberately wallowed in 'the rubbish of departed ignorance' and raked up 'the ashes of dead savages to find gewgaws and rattles for the grown babies of the age'. Byron, Scott, Southey, Wordsworth, Coleridge came under fire from Peacock in his denunciation of backwardness and triviality. 'Mr Wordsworth picks up village legends from old women and sextons; and Mr Coleridge, to the valuable information acquired from similar sources, superadds the dreams of crazy theologians and the mysticisms of German metaphysics, and favours the world with visions in verse, in which the quadruple elements of sexton, old woman, Jeremy Taylor, and Immanuel Kant, are harmonized into a delicious poetical compound . . . '

Peacock's *Four Ages* appeared in *Ollier's Literature Miscellany* in 1820, and Sir Henry Taylor's manifesto served as Preface to *Philip van Artevelde* in 1834. The years between form a singularly colourless period of our literary history. By 1830 the Romantic Movement had faded into emotional apathy. Such poets as were writing seemed to be sensible, dull fellows, and prose too was heavy and verbose. 'Providence warns me to have done with literature,' wrote Carlyle in 1835, and a couple of years later he was talking of buying a gun and a spade and taking himself off to the American wilds. Tennyson, who was too late to be a great Romantic and too soon to be a great Pre-Raphaelite, discovered that he had been born at exactly the wrong moment and remained silent for ten years after his first two volumes in 1830 and 1833.

Not that there were no poets around, but the general atmosphere was curiously unfavourable to the birth of any but the most trivial verse. With the departure of the splendid muscularity of Byron, there seemed to be nothing new to read but Felicia Hemans and Laetitia Landon of the Keepsake style, together with oddities like Beddoes, Darley, and the imaginary Oriental translations of James Clarence Mangan. There was no lack of lengthy, not to say pretentious, poems, which sold enormously. Robert Montgomery's *Omnipresence of the Deity* and Robert Pollok's *Course of Time* sold eight editions and over a hundred-thousand copies respectively. One gains the impression that the public was buying the commodity by the yard. Martin Tupper's enormously successful *Proverbial Philosophy*, selling well over a hundred-thousand copies, presaged the mass-production of Victorian industry. 'This unbounded indulgence in the mere luxuries of poetry', as Sir Henry Taylor called it, certainly justified his complaint of the 'inadequate appreciation of its intellectual part'. There had been occasional superabundance in verse in the eighteenth century, with Dr Darwin's *Botanic Garden,* and Dyer's celebration of the textile trades in *The Fleece*. Now it was pouring from the presses in a spate of mere productivity.

'Men are grown mechanical in head and in heart, as well as in hand,' Carlyle declared in his essay 'Signs of the Times' which he wrote for the *Edinburgh Review* in 1829 . . . 'let us observe how the mechanical genius of our time has diffused itself into quite other provinces. Not the external and physical alone is now managed by machinery, but the internal and spiritual also.' He didn't actually say that poetry was now produced by machinery. Indeed, it seems, from examination of some of the lengthier poems of the time, that they would have been greatly improved by a touch of the computer, had that benign engine existed. Charles Babbage was already working on his calculating-machine, the 'small engine model' being much talked about in the early 'twenties. It is something of a stroke of irony that the year of William IV's death was the year when Philip James Bailey retired to his father's house at Basford, close by Nottingham, the seat of the lace-trade, in order to compose his vast poem, *Festus*. For *Festus* bore all the features that Sir Henry Taylor deplored, along with a number of the features whose absence he regretted. While it was exciting, in places frenetic, full of 'invocations', cries of acclaim (it opened with a chorus-cry of 'God! God! God!'—invocatory rather than expletive)—it made a considerable show of intellectual content, for (as someone said of Milton) 'Bailey made God argue'. No one in his senses expects poets to write in accordance with manifestos, or the rule-books of critics, and it may be doubted whether Philip Bailey up in Basford among the lace-makers was even aware that Sir Henry Taylor had delivered his caveat against that kind of thing, and it is pretty certain that a hundred Sir Henry's would not have deterred him from writing the way he did. After he had written of how **God the** Creator

> sowed with seeds of light what we call worlds
> The boundless and the barren fields of space,

he read in *Paradise Lost* that the Deity had 'sowed the Heavens with stars thick as a field' and at once erased his own words, but he confessed that he found consolation in having thought what Milton thought. There was no false modesty about Philip Bailey. He addresses the reader with the calm assurance of an immortal, and Helen begs him to go on talking after he has delivered many lines of *Festus* for her benefit.

> Do let me hear;
> Thy talk is the sweet extracts of all speech,
> And holds mine ear in blissful slavery.

The reader would hesitate to say the same. Bailey was only twenty when he wrote *Festus*, although it is true that he went on writing it all his life. As a satirist said:

> He sang himself hoarse to the stars very early
> And cracked a weak voice with too lofty a tune.

To be lofty was thought to be the poet's characteristic stance in those days. There was no more certain way of producing lowly poetry.

It may be, of course, that the best energies of the Early Victorians—at least, what there was to spare after creating the Menai Bridge and Euston Station—went into prose. It is often difficult to distinguish the prose from the poetry of that time, and even lawyer-like critics, James Fitzjames Stephen for instance, were apt to use the two terms interchangeably. Bentham had once remarked that the only difference between poetry and prose was the fact that in poetry the first and the last lines alone come up to the margin, while in prose they all do. His disciple, Fitzjames Stephen, once quoted a passage from Carlyle's *Sartor Resartus* as 'the most memorable utterance of the age's greatest poet'. The passage on the toilworn craftsman in the fourth chapter of the third book can be scanned like poetry, and if this (as some have averred) makes it bad prose, it is only necessary to read it in order to refute the view. Nor is it only a matter of scansion and 'poetic' language. It is more importantly a matter of energy. There is among the writers of verse in the period between the death of Keats and the prime of Tennyson and Browning a singular lack of drive, or dynamics. It is not that their verse lacks energy in line or stanza. It is rather that it lacks the permeative power that turns a string of verses into a poem. Permeative power of that order is not like the glue or the nails that belong to carpentry. It is an all-pervasive presence. Perhaps there is little that can be said in the last analysis except that the age was somewhat short on genius.

CHAPTER 6

The Coming of the Railway

'I CON-SIDER,' said Mr Weller, 'that the rail is unconstitutional, and an inwader of privileges. . . . '

William IV gave his name to a famous locomotive, but he never rode with Puffing Billy, and 'the railway Age' did not properly arrive until after his death. Nor did the railway language which made 'getting up steam' and similar locutions into household terms, nor did the governing of men's lives by the temporal tyranny of Mr Bradshaw begin until the reign of Victoria. The first of the great London termini was opened at Euston Square in 1838, the year after the Queen's accession. 1837 saw also the patenting of the electric telegraph, a means of communication historically inseparable from the railways. The age of the stage-coach had not been long before it was swept into the transport-museum. It is only remembered fondly on table-mats and coloured prints in hotels because it possessed so many attractive appurten-ances, post-horses, post-horns, multi-caped coachmen, all the jolly furniture of the Dickens novel. 'Puffing Billy', however reminiscent of the King, could not compete. What Chesterton called 'the rank, rowdy tradition of men falling off coaches' was now to give place to the Sons of Science travelling primly on rails or in grooves. George Borrow was a boy of sixteen in the year of Peterloo, and he was thirty-four when Queen Victoria came to the throne. The great records of the England of the Romany Rye and Jasper Petulengro belong to the 1850's, the mid-Victorian years, when their world had faded into darkness. Who would imagine that *Lavengro* came out in the year of the Great Exhibition?

The coming of the railways meant that ordinary Englishmen and women came to see and thereby to know their country for the

1 Jeremy Bentham

2 Samuel Coleridge

3 Humphrey Davy

4 William Lamb,
  2nd Viscount
  Melbourne

5 Henry Brougham
  (*from a portrait by
  Lonsdale*)

6 King William IV in 1839 (after Wivell)

7 Charles, 2nd Earl Grey (after Lawrence)

8 King's Cross Station, the London terminus of the G.N.R.,
designed by Lewis Cubitt.

9 'Puffing Billy' the Wylam Colliery locomotive
built in 1813 under William Hedley's patent.

first time. Heretofore they had seen England, if at all, from the back of a horse, like Celia Fiennes or William Cobbett, or like those prize pedestrians—Samuel Bamford or William Holcroft. The great multitude never saw anything beyond the parish boundaries. 'Railroad travelling is a delightful improvement of human life,' said Sydney Smith when the great change had come. 'Everything is near, everything is immediate—time, distance, delay are abolished.' Excursion-trains were running by 1840, and Mr Thomas Cook was busy by 1841. Thousands were carried up to the Great Exhibition ten years later for a few shillings apiece. 'Where will they find shoes?' the Duke of Wellington had asked with some satisfaction when in 1832 it was reported that fifty thousand men were travelling to London from Birmingham with a petition in support of the Reform Bill. Ten years later the Birmingham Radicals were enraged by the transport of a contingent of the Metropolitan Police by railway-train to their city in order to contend with Chartist demonstrations. It was 'unconstitutional' they said. Hitherto, down the centuries, provincial rioters had always had twenty-four hours' start of London's peace-keeping forces. That was one thing that railways had put an end to. Not only was rural disorder far harder to bring about without interference, but people knew it was.

There was, however, one kind of demonstration that the railway had little chance of affecting, and this was the activities of Captain Swing, the latest version of King Ludd. Cobbett was fond of boasting of the effect of his own works, more especially his *History of the Protestant Reformation,* [in a *Series of Letters addressed to all Sensible and Just Englishmen*] (1824–7) and *The Poor Man's Friend* (1826) upon the Swing men, thrashers, hedgers, ditchers, ploughmen, mowers and reapers who had turned their attention to the destruction of agricultural machinery as their predecessors had destroyed stocking-frames. People were not formidable when assembled together in great towns, Cobbett held, 'it was not until the month of October, 1830, when the chopsticks set about the work that I really expected it (Parliamentary Reform) to come in any reasonable time'. Urban meetings and petitions did a certain amount of good, 'but the great and efficient cause (i.e. of Reform) was the movements of the chopsticks', by which he meant the agricultural labourers. Certainly the powers-that-be were always most alarmed, and most savagely repressive, when the farm-workers went into action, as may be seen from the relentless treatment of the Dorchester labourers, or 'the Tolpuddle Martyrs'. Neither the 'Whiff-of-Grapeshot' treatment (which was never tried in England), nor the Peterloo type of action, had any chance of subduing men who struck in lonely places and disappeared into the darkness of field and woodland. To that extent Cobbett's claim to superiority for the countryman in revolutionary action was probably justified, though we may discount his claim for the tremendous influence of his own writings and speeches in 1830. 'If you could have heard one of these', he boasted, 'you could not wonder that the nation was roused, that all spoke as one man, and that we now have that Reform which the nation owes to those lectures more than to all other causes put together.' After all it was not Cobbett but Samuel Bamford who had said in 1816 when the price of *The Political Register* was reduced to twopence (thus literally becoming 'The Tuppenny Trash') that it was read on every cottage hearth in the manufacturing districts and that 'riots soon became scarce'. When the old man claimed for his later writings and speeches that they had been the principal agency for parliamentary reform he was claiming the success of what he had been trying to effect throughout his career. It is sad to see and hear the ageing heroes of the people's cause as the world moves on-ward. Some of them seem to sigh for the 'Good Old Days' when the field rang with the war-cries of another and a better generation. Borrow, while he was never much of a politician and could not remember many years back beyond Peterloo, called the penulti-mate chapter of his *Lavengro*, 'Pseudo-Radicals', explaining that their time was from 1820 to 1832. The only Radicals he has a good word for are the leaders of the Cato Street Plot. The others were humbugs, prepared for any dirty job which might get them a place.

> This very dirty man, with his very dirty face,
> Would do any dirty act, which would get him a place.

It is a commonplace that the railways, like other changes in modes of communication, caused the world to shrink, so people could no longer plead ignorance of each other and of unfamiliar ways of life. While the great spate of Blue Books revealed 'how the other half lived', the opening up of the country by the railways brought unfamiliar facts of life under men's eyes. Not only did men and woman come to see and thereby know their country. They came to know and see each other. Mr Weller was alarmed to think that a middle-aged gentleman might find himself 'locked up in a close carriage vith a living widder' who, he was convinced, would have married him before they reached the next station if there had been a clergyman in the conweyance. Nor was it only a question of physical proximity. It was a matter of changes in the style of human living. The late Humphrey House was able to show, by quoting the Home Office Papers, that the appearance, dress, and manner of 'the younger Watson' who was taken up for his part in the Spa Fields riot of December, 1817, bore a detailed similarity to the early Dickens characters (i.e. those of *Pickwick, Oliver Twist, Nicholas Nickleby* and *The Old Curiosity Shop*), all of which appeared between 1837 and 1840. After that a different style appears not only in places and things but in persons. They have become 'modern'. House was confident that this new mood and atmosphere were very largely brought about by the railways, which changed not only the landscape but 'the scope and tempo of individual living'. Professor Clive Lewis called it 'the greatest change in the history of western man', as mighty as the change from stone to bronze, or from a pastoral to an agricultural economy. It was epochal.

Epochal changes of life-style are sometimes accompanied by singularly trivial changes in the styles of clothes. The first considerable writer to expatiate upon sartorial changes in a philosophical way was Thomas Carlyle, whose 'Sartor Resartus' was written in 1831. Unfortunately Carlyle almost entirely omits to discourse upon the style in hats. The style in hats, however, becomes peculiarly significant at this time, falling as it does between the handsome and the hideous, the cocked-hat of the Georgians and the chimney-pot 'tile' of the Victorians. The strange headgear of the post-Georgians or the pre-Victorians, whichever way one may choose to look at it, seems to suggest that the men of that intermediary age had lost their way. The style somewhat resembles the tall hat worn by a chef, and also reminds one of a German University student's casque. It may be seen in portraits of William Corder who was hanged in 1828 at Bury St Edmunds for the murder of Maria Marten. Corder was a vain young man and it may be taken for granted that he would wear, even in Bury Gaol, what he thought was the latest style. Young men and boys are to be seen wearing such hats in the background of the illustrations of William Howitt's *Boy's Country Book* (1839). So too the overseer superintending the power-looms in J. Tingle's industrial engraving of a factory loom-shop in 1835. Sometimes these hats resemble the 'mortar-board' of academic costume, and they seem oddly out of place in a world of increasing mechanisation. Never was a style so short-lived, perhaps because it was so inappropriate to the world of 'business'. The stove-pipe hat of the early Victorians which looks as if it came straight off 'Puffing Billy' or Stephenson's 'Rocket' is far more in character. Thomas de Quincey whose 'Murder as a Fine Art' first appeared in *Blackwood's Magazine* in 1827, the year of the murder of Maria Marten in the Red Barn, would have been the authority to consult.

Life-styles are only the converse of death-styles, and every age has its own style in the art of murder. Murders in the period between Peterloo and Victoria were peculiarly ghastly. First there was John Thurtell, the 'flash-cove' from Norwich, and acquaintance of George Borrow who watched him among the prize-fighters on Mousehold Heath. He was hanged for the murder of William Weare at Elstree in 1822. A popular song gleefully celebrated his crime:

> They cut his throat from ear to ear,
> His brains they battered in,
> His name was Mr William Weare,
> He lived in Lincoln's Inn.

Not long after this, the man-servant, Courvoisier, cut the throat of his master, Lord William Russell, as he lay in bed early one morning. Cutting throats, a straight-forward if bloody way of slaying people, was the style just then. Poisoning set in with the Rugely poisoner, Dr Palmer, in 1856, and proved to be the style of the Victorian Age. Why? It was tidier, and superficially less brutal than the knife, or the pistol, more civilized. The lowest point had been reached with James Blomfield Rush in 1849, whose performance at Stanfield Hall near Norwich had a wholesale and totally un-English character, though Rush was a Norfolk farmer and thought to have been much influenced by reading the ultra-English William Cobbett. But there are no firm rules. The classic railway-murder had to wait for the German, Franz Muller, who slew Mr Thompson on the Brighton line in 1879. He was detected, and finally hanged, because he lost his hat in the process, giving his name to the low-crowned 'hard' hat, which was for long known as 'Muller-cut-down', contracted into the single word 'Muller-cudown'. It never really caught on, however, like the Corder-casque.

Two other features which specially characterised the Victorian Age had as yet given only premonitions of their arrival. One is the cult of nonsense which showed itself with the publication of Edward Lear's first *Book of Nonsense* in 1846. Lear is so well-remembered as a Victorian that it occurs to few people that he was, like so many other great Victorians, a child of the Regency. The first thing he remembered was being taken from his bed in a blanket in order to look out of the window of his father's house on Highgate Hill to see the illuminations down in London for the Battle of Waterloo. When he published his first Nonsense Book he said that he had had no ulterior motive, political, satirical, or anything else. 'Nonsense', he said, 'pure and absolute, having been my aim throughout'. Of course, Lear did not invent the limerick, but he sent it on its way as an art-form so splendidly that there were already two schools of thought on the rhyming of the last line before he died. The other classic exponent of nonsense, Lewis Carroll, was in fact an intellectual pioneer of lunatic logic, which is a very different thing from Lear's 'pure and absolute nonsense'. For one thing it had far less to do with poetry. Lear's 'Nonsense Songs' did not begin to appear until the eighteen-seventies, a fact which in itself guarantees their profoundly serious character. It would probably be possible to show that this was where the missing poetry of the 'thirties had got to, just as the missing music of the whole Victorian Age went underground like the Mozartian stream that gushed forth in the latter years of the century with Arthur Sullivan in the Savoy Operas.

The other feature which began to show itself now was 'the Country-book', a peculiarly English phenomenon which developed into the Victorian tradition of 'rural writings'. This kind of work is to be distinguished from the gentlemanly amateurism of Gilbert White, and springs rather from the wholesome journalism of professional writers like William Howitt. Howitt made the country writing yield him a steady income for many years. '*The Boy's Country Book*' was composed in 1839, and evidently portrays rural life in England under William IV. Howitt had the good fortune to be born in the border-land between Derbyshire and Nottinghamshire where the ploughman's whistle mingled with the rattle of colliery-gear. His father was a small farmer who combined farming with colliery-management at the remote little township of Heanor. 'Boyhood in the country! Paradise of opening existence! . . . With that charming country all around me, I was an Adam in Eden . . . ' This little book breathes the nostalgia of a country boy who has seen the countryside shrink before the creeping advance of an industrial, predominantly urban society. What makes Howitt's book so fascinating is his awareness, as long ago as the reign of William IV, of 'the world we have lost'. Now, more than a century since *The Boy's Country Book* was published, its scenes are entombed as deep beneath the bus-routes and council-houses of the 'awful Erewash Valley' as D. H. Lawrence, another of its children, called it, as Herculaneum beneath its lava. To see it in proper perspective, Howitt's *Country Book* needs to be read in the Heanor of today. It is like listening to the distant voice of the waves in a shell picked up on the shore of a sea which long ago swallowed a whole world. That world was still all around the men and women of the age between Peterloo and the reign of Queen Victoria, but they were already beginning to write valedictory books about it.

Best of all Thomas Bewick had already immortalised it in his wood-engravings. He had drawn his *Quadrupeds* (1790) and his two volumes of *British Birds* (1797 and 1804). Magnificent as many of these are, they are less interesting to the historian than are his tail-pieces and his vignettes of the human scene, where we catch magical glimpses of the rural world in the days of William Cobbett. 'I have heard those who loved the country', Howitt wrote in 1844, 'and loved it because they knew it, say, that the opening of Bewick was a new era in their lives.' It surely has been so ever since, and will be when the earth is one sheet of tarmac.

CHAPTER 7

The New Radicals

THOMAS BEWICK was a Radical and a Deist, and he was these things after the fashion of a good Geordie, or Northcountry-man, that is to say as part of his character. Not for him the imbibing of the gospel according to Godwin, or even Tom Paine, but the discovery of truth by personal experience, 'proved on the pulses'. Edmund Blunden once said, 'a good naturalist cannot be a bad man', and Bewick 'quite simply saw his own exemplary life as a demonstration of that'. The fact is that he qualified as an early Victorian by his smugness. So, by the way did Cobbett especially in his *Advice to Young Men*, and particularly in his advice about choosing a wife. What had happened to the Radical since the days of Bamford and Benbow, Baggaley and Drummond? Perhaps it was the Methodist streak or the Evangelical leaven. Some would call it a taint.

It is always better to talk of Radicals rather than of Radicalism. The subject is best treated in a nominalist fashion, for all Radicals are different, idiosyncracy being their characteristic feature. That is one reason why there has never been a Radical Party for every Radical tends to be a party to himself. The Radical lives for difference and distinction. There is no need to pay any attention to the animadversions of George Borrow with his suggestion that the only thing the post–1820 Radicals could not get in their pursuit of the Main Chance was rich husbands for their ugly daughters. This ungallant conclusion is hardly surprising in the man who tells us that he spent his time in Mumper's Dingle coaching Isobel Berners in linguistics. Probably the pattern of the species after 1820 is Francis Place, that grey, mole-like character whom Cobbett for long suspected as a government-spy. Prolonged contact with the multitudinous Place Papers at the British Museum turned even

that humane and human scholar, Graham Wallas, into something
of a bore when he came to write his *Life of Place*, or was it only the
effect of his association with the Fabians? Place's career, however,
belonged to both the early and the later periods of Radicalism in
London, his life extending from 1771 to 1854. A more convincing
pattern of the Radical species after 1820 is probably to be found
in William Lovett, who was not born until 1800 and was not
engaged in Radical politics until 1825. There were among them,
too, some veterans of the seventeen-nineties, men like Ernest Gale
Jones who handed down the tradition of the early and dangerous
days to the Radicals of the Rotunda in Blackfriars Bridge Road
where the great meetings of the National Union of the Working
Classes were held in 1831. Here is one of the main links between
the London Corresponding Society and the Chartists. 'A poor
emaciated, crazy-looking creature', is his description in the *Place
Papers*, and Burdetts, the Lord Williams and the Lord Henries
and the Lord Charleses, and, in short, the whole family; 'I have
seen them, all these, all the same faces and names, all my life-time'.

It is always pleasing to the historian to see history repeating
itself, which it frequently does, although the repetitions are rarely
exact enough to be useful for the purposes of prophesy. When the
London Corresponding Society drew up its Address to the Inhabitants of Great Britain on the subject of Parliamentary Reform
in August 1792, they linked political with economic reform.
Indeed, they were intent on making reform a 'knife-and-fork'
question from the beginning: how were they to interest the working man in it? The conjunction of knives-and forks with ballot-
boxes returned in full force in the era of the Great Reform Bill.
The movement for the People's Charter, Six Points and all, which
was published in 1838, was only superficially political. The pur
pose of the Six Points—manhood suffrage, vote by ballot, annual
parliaments, abolition of property qualification of M.P.s etc.—
was to forge weapons for the transformation of society into a
Socialist Commonwealth. Whatever the Reform Bill may have
achieved it had very little to do with social justice. Even as regards
the extension of the franchise it was seemingly irrelevant to any
wider purpose than a scant political adjustment. Sometimes it even
reduced the franchise, as in Orator Hunt's constituency at Preston,

where hundreds of pot-wallopers lost the suffrage while a few £10 householders gained it. Radicals on the whole had accepted the Reform Bill on the principle that half a loaf was better than no bread, and in confidence as men liked to say, that once Parliament had been reformed 'all else shall be added unto you'. The 'Feast of the Barmecide' which followed it made a great many Radicals into Socialists, prepared now to become Chartists in order to bring about the further political reform which was evidently the precondition of economic and social amelioration.

Whigs, and intellectual Radicals, were on the whole less enthusiastic in their attitude to Socialist ideas than were Tories. There has always been a certain affinity between Socialism and Toryism, indeed Herbert Spencer more than once called Socialism 'the New Toryism'. Philosophic Radicalism of the Benthamite variety was closely associated with laissez-faire economics, and regarded the intrusion of the State into the economic sphere as complete heresy. Nothing enraged a man like James Mill, Jeremy Bentham's principal disciple, more than the propagation of Socialist ideas among the working-men. 'Nothing can be more mischievous', he wrote in a letter to Lord Brougham in 1832 alluding to the labour theory of value as 'the mad nonsense of our friend Hodgskin,* which he has published as a system and propagates with the zeal of perfect fanaticism'. The triumph of such ideas, Mill thought, would have worse effects than 'the overwhelming deluge of Huns and Tartars'. He was glad to say that he had never met a labouring-man ('and I have tried the experiment upon many of them') whom he had failed to convince that the existence of private property was more beneficial to the working class than to any other. The trouble was that there were too many cheap publications which preached such mischievous doctrines as the right of the labouring people ('Who they say are the only producers') to all that is produced. The alarming nature of this evil might be understood when one reflected that these publications were superseding the Sunday newspapers and every other channel through which the people might get better information.

While the argument proceeded over what Mill called 'the mad

*Thomas Hodgskin, 1783–1869, *Labour defended against the Claims of Capital, or the Unproductiveness of Capital proved*, (1825).

nonsense' concerning labour's right to the whole product, con-
stituting an angry controversy in the Chartist movement, one
practical Socialist, who was also an active philanthropist, was
getting on with the task of exhibiting a paternalistic type of
Socialism in action. Robert Owen instituted his model community
at New Lanark where he possessed the chief interest in some
cotton mills, attracting thither the eyes, and some of the enthusiasm, of utopians. New Lanark was the cynosure of many eyes,
as Thomas Coke's Holkham had been earlier in the realm of
agriculture. People visited New Lanark from all over Europe,
even from Russia, the model being publicised not only by Owen's
writings, which were numerous and widely-read, but by such
public figures as Lord Liverpool, the Prime Minister from 1812
to 1827, who had circulated Owen's ideas among the representa-
tives of the powers assembled for the Congress of Vienna. The
rumour had gone around that Robert Owen had solved the social
problem of poverty and the oppressive burden of poor-rates. At
any rate Tories like the Poet Laureate, Robert Southey, urged an
open mind on the question. 'As to Owen', we find him writing in
1816, 'he is far gone in metaphysics, but neither rogue nor mad-
man. *We must see Lanark* before we can fairly appreciate what he
has done.' Whether he went personally and, if so, what he found,
is not certain, but two English Quakers, William and Mary
Howitt, called while travelling in Scotland on their honeymoon,
in 1822, and, fortunately for their objectivity, Robert Owen
happened to be away at the time, and they were able to talk freely
to the workers. The honest report of such visitors is far more
valuable than second-hand descriptions of visitors engaged in
conducted-tours. They found the factory-children most unruly at
lessons, and enquired whether the masters ever flogged them.
'No,' was the answer from the teacher, 'It is contrary to Mr Owen's
system.' The answer of the pupils, when no one was listening was:
'Joost sometimes.' The visitors commented that the workers
seemed to have a very pleasant place, and must be very happy. To
which the reply was, 'Why, very well, very well . . . ' To the
remark that New Lanark had been most talked about in distant
places, they replied: 'Ay, the further off the more talked about, I
dare say.' As for the comfort of living in the quiet and orderly

little village, the reply was 'if a man drinks or thieves, he must be marching, but there are other things besides these, enough to prevent the place from being too pleasant'. Why then did they stay? It was a long way to the next factory. What about wages? 'Small, small,' they said. But such was the excellence of Mr Owen's system, and such his care for the future of their children, surely that made up for everything? The comment on this was, 'Mr Owen has a many fine notions, but, though it is treason to say it, 'tis but patching up poor human nature, that, if it be stopped in one place, will break out in another.'

When Cobbett visited New Lanark he got the impression that Owen's system inculcated habits of implicit submission, and there is no doubt that Owen was very much of a dictator, even if he was a completely benevolent one, which is doubtless the reason why he attained the considerable degree of success that he did in a society where insubordination had always been the rule and where the rank and file of employees had always preferred to go to hell in their own way rather than to heaven in someone else's. Fortunately Owen's future reputation among the workers depended less upon the extremely shaky attachment to democracy than upon his practice of a certain rough and ready syndicalism, eventuating in the Trade Union Movement and the associated Co-operative Society. Much of Owen's work was vitiated by his fanatical devotion to certain nostrums like 'Man's character is made for, and not by, him', maxims which dominated the fundamentally uneducated mind of the great philanthropist and by constant reiteration precluded the painful process of further thought. One corollary of his dogmatic environmentalism was equally dogmatic rejection of Christianity, a course which cost him the support of most thinking men and women, quite apart from 'interested parties' in the clergy. As the years passed he became more and more of a millenarian, writing endless books on revolutionising the mind and practice of the Human Race. He ended up, as might have been expected, as a Spiritualist, with the ghosts of Jefferson, Metternich, and Napoleon among his proselytes. He also claimed to have converted the father of the future Queen Victoria, the Duke of Kent, to necessitarian Socialism. His Royal Highness managed to borrow several hundred pounds from Owen, and never paid him back, though Owen may have thought himself repaid by the Duke's consenting to preside at one of his public meetings and later corresponding with him from the spirit-world in terms which Owen found gratifying to his own Socialist sentiments, for instance to the effect that there were no titles in the spiritual sphere where he now resided.

The idiosyncratic character of the Radicals as the reign of Queen Victoria succeeded to the reigns of the sons of George III probably had a good deal to do with the fact that they enjoyed a plenitude of the world's wealth. How rich must one be in order to furnish the means to a milder madness? The world in general seems to have taken it for granted that if Victorian Englishmen liked to make themselves uncomfortable by holding Radical opinions, they must be on the whole a little cracked, and was prepared to tolerate it because they enjoyed a long purse. Nor were wealthy Radicals, from Robert Owen down to Wilfrid Scawen Blunt and Cunningham Grahame any exception. The less wealthy, possessing no such excuse, simply went on working hard and talking nonsense with the impunity of the unimportant. Some of them did their best to get into trouble, but for the most part kept out of jail—and the madhouse. William Howitt, the Quaker who kept the druggist's shop at the lower corner of the Exchange in Nottingham Market-place, was one of these. He and Mary, his wife, gave the hospitality of Friends to William Wordsworth when the poet was in Nottingham in the summer of 1831.

'The Wordsworths left them full of gratitude for their kindness', wrote Southey, 'and full of liking for Mary. But her husband, whom they might otherwise have liked much, (though never quite so well) had the Reform fever upon him . . . '

William, the apple-cheeked, flaxen-haired little character from Heanor, offended the visitors by exulting in the prospect of the downfall of the Church with the savagery of a Dissenter who had forgotten that he was a Quaker and a man of peace. Mary, his wife, made him apologize to the Wordsworths afterwards. But, as Robert Southey comments when telling the story of the fracas, 'the circumstance shows what these sectarians are when the latent spirit is brought out.'

The latent spirit that fired William Howitt was that of a people who had for long been an oppressed minority. This experience of social, and political, exclusion from the 'establishment' played no inconsiderable part in swelling the ranks of the English Radicals. What, they asked rather understandably had they to lose by dislodging the powers that be? They exulted in the first successful blow delivered by the Great Reform Bill. Despite their Quakerly pacifism they must have found it hard not to rejoice when Nottingham Castle went up in flames on that October night in 1831 on the news reaching the town that the House of Lords had thrown out the Bill. William and Mary viewed the fiery scene from the leads of their house beside the Market-place, and William's account of the conflagration remains the best eye-witness description of the occasion. Militant Dissenters were numerous in Nottingham, and their Radicalism contained a strong anti-clerical element. When the Reform Bill was at last passed the Nottingham Radicals kept up their agitation at the expense of the established Church which, they rightly considered, had been the ecclesiastical ally of the unreformed Parliament.

Scarcely were the embers of Nottingham Castle cold when William Howitt sat down to compose his *Popular History of Priestcraft in all Ages and Nations*. Its publication, wrote his wife, 'turned William almost overnight into a Radical politician, and a public character in Nottingham'. He was at once drawn more and more into Radical and anti-clerical warfare. Soon he was elected an alderman, and was sent to London with a petition asking for the disestablishment of the Church. This is the point at which the country-boy from Heanor emerges for a brief moment upon the larger page of his country's history. He and his companions waited upon Earl Grey who listened sympathetically to their statement of grievances as Dissenters in the matter of their disabilities, but the P.M. made it quite clear that the Government would have nothing to do with 'destruction of the Establishment'. Supposing their disabilities were removed, Lord Grey seems to say, surely his petitioners would not wish to do away with all established religion? Aye, said William Howitt, that was precisely what they had come about. At least, both parties now knew where they stood. Earl Grey, it is clear, had always known. William

Howitt, one suspects, had imagined that he had only to show a rational gentleman like Earl Grey that the Dissenter suffered disabilities because of the Establishment and he would set himself to abolish it. The visit to Downing Street showed him that this was a fallacy. There was no question of the walls of Jericho falling at a shout. They stood intact all William's life. They stand intact still. It had been a lesson in how things were, and are, and must be, the first—perhaps the only—lesson that adult life teaches.

The Howitts, man and wife, had been through the fire of experience, without a lick of flame, although their friends seem to have enjoyed the notion of their martyrdom. 'Some people do say that William will be cited before the House of Lords', Mary told the Friends; 'others that he will be imprisoned in the Tower'. A kind Tory friend in London had written offering to take her and the children into her house while William was in the Tower, and was even trying to arrange for them to visit him there. Of course there was not the slightest danger. No one could possibly have imagined the little volume in its drab covers contained a grain of dynamite. It quickly went into a second edition. It was pirated in an abridged form. The Mechanics' Institute bought it. In fact William enjoyed a modest celebrity, which may have helped to carry off better works like his *Boy's Country Book* and *The Rural Life of England*. Indeed it may be said to have sent both William and Mary on their modest, but not unlucrative course, as flourishing figures of the Victorian literary scene. They were recruited by Charles Dickens for *Household Words* and for the Annuals, Tait's *Edinburgh Magazine*, and many another repository of domestic literature. None of their multifarious works have survived in the common memory, unless one excepts Mary's little poems for infants, *The Spider and the Fly* and *The Squirrels*. William's journalism contains many records of rural life worth looking at in *Visits to Remarkable Places,* and *Homes and Haunts of the British Poets*. 'William-and-Mary' constitute a conglomerate figure in Victorian England, not only in its lower literature but in its respectable Radicalism. Mary worked with the pioneers of the higher education of women like Barbara Bodichon, and ended her life in the bosom of the Roman Church—after William's death.

CHAPTER 8

Thomas Bailey

IT WAS a great day for Mary Howitt when she saw the tall rather gaunt figure of William Wordsworth hurrying across Nottingham Market Place to knock on the door of William Howitt the druggist. His wife had been struck down by the lumbago on the way from London to Rydal Mount. Still greater was Mary Howitt's delight to have 'the greatest poet of the age' seated with her William in the front parlour over the shop while the two of them talked the sun up with their speculations about 'the future prospects of society and all subjects connected with poetry and the interests of man'. This was the occasion on which William Howitt put his foot in it by exulting in the prospect of the downfall of the Church, asserting that anyone who was a clergyman of the Establishment must be either a fool or a hypocrite, a remark which caused Dora, whose brother and uncle were clergymen, to leave the room in some haste. Wordsworth himself had always been fundamentally a Radical, even declaring that while he despised the Whigs he always felt there was much of the Chartist in him, but William Howitt ought to have remembered that he was talking in the presence of the author of *Ecclesiastical Sonnets*.

With a younger Nottingham poet, Philip Bailey, William Howitt consorted with less embarrassment. This young man used to drop in at the Howitt's fireside of an evening with the manuscript of *Festus* in his pocket and read from it endlessly while the wind howled round the Market Place and over the roof-tops while the Quaker-chemist and his wife lifted their eyes and their hands in wondering admiration. Young Philip was one of their own sort, the ardent son of a provincial merchant who had a wholesale business at the bottom of Friar Lane. Thomas Bailey was brought up, like his father before him, in the hosiery trade, the typical business of a solid middle-class native of Nottingham. But it was the wine-trade that enabled him to attain to the substantial social and economic status that he came to enjoy in the town, and especially to acquire Basford House in the country nearby. He also acquired the *Nottingham Mercury*, the official Whig newspaper, although his possession of it lasted only some five years, as the organ of his moderate and middleclass views. There was in Thomas Bailey, however, a high degree of literary ability, whence may have originated the outstanding literary gifts of his son. He sent Philip to the Free School, and thence to the University of Glasgow where he trained for the legal profession. Like his father, but with greater intensity, Philip was always scribbling poetry. He never practised as a lawyer, and Glasgow made him an Honorary LLD, in absentia when he was over eighty. What really pleased him, no doubt, was the move to get him made poet laureate after Tennyson in 1892 when he was seventy-six. Thirty-six years had passed since he had been called 'the last and possibly the greatest of our English poets'. It is rare to find anyone, even in Philip Bailey's own land, who has ever read *Festus*. A poet, like a prophet, is not without honour . . .

Thomas Bailey certainly never attained honour beyond the boundaries of his native town, but his son Philip was to be famous in the New World as well as the Old long into the nineteenth century. This may be more than a little unjust, for Thomas Bailey's work, *The Annals of Nottinghamshire*, published in 1853, when he was sixty-eight, is an example of those local histories for whose excellence the Victorian Age is no less worthy of honour than it is for the national histories of Green and Macaulay. It is true that Thomas Bailey confined himself to 'Annals', and he would probably have been puzzled, even sceptical, if anyone had enquired about his 'philosophy' of history. Like a good citizen, like Thucydides at Athens, or Guicciardini at Florence, he wanted to set down what had happened, and especially what he had seen happen in his own lifetime, which is the oldest, and even now the most worthwhile form of history. He had witnessed history in the making in one of history's most lively fields for more than sixty lively years. Nottingham occupied, and occupies, almost the midpoint of England. Brooding there under the tawny rock crowned

c

by the castle like an Acropolis, although everyone knows it is only the cube-like home of the Duke of Newcastle, crouching like the people of Lilliput between the claws of a lion asleep in the sunshine, and very well aware that the beast might awaken at any moment, Nottingham has always had the startled aspect of a revolutionary city. Such was its popular reputation for disorder that the question one used to ask of anyone who came from Nottingham was: 'had any good riots lately?' Not only was Nottingham the centre of the machine-wreckers, the capital of King Ludd, it was the town where the very magistrates and city-fathers were famous for their Radicalism. 'The Paris of the Midlands', was its nickname. Men said that what Paris did yesterday, Nottingham does today and England will do tomorrow. It had seen the first act of war in 1642 when King Charles had raised his standard in the Castle courtyard. It had seen Lucy Hutchinson and her husband, the Colonel, holding the castle for the Parliament, and Henry Ireton riding in from Attenborough, sword in hand. Thomas Bailey celebrated Henry Ireton, Cromwell's fiery son-in-law, as Robert Browning celebrated Thomas Wentworth, Earl of Strafford, at much the same time. While Nottingham led the nation in arms and in the assault upon stocking-frames, Nottingham followed the rest of the nation in poetry even while it had Byron close at hand. By the opening of Queen Victoria's reign did Nottingham think perhaps that it was high time she gave England her modern epic-poet? It is rare nowadays to meet anyone who has read, or perhaps ever heard of *Festus*. Probably most people imagine that Festus was the poet's Christian name. *Festus* was certainly the work of his life, for he was adding to it throughout the Victorian Age. He even called his only son who was in the Nottingham Post Office for many years, 'Festus'. That was the boy whom Dame Laura Knight, a neighbour, played with as a child though she did not, unfortunately, paint his portrait. The Poet himself was painted as a young man by another local artist, Robert James, and his bust in black basalt gazes out from the Castle, occupying a niche next to William Howitt. David Herbert Lawrence, a vastly superior man of letters, would make a more convincing memorial in that gallery than either of them.

It seems more than a little unjust that Thomas Bailey should be remembered only as the father of Philip, or Festus. True, he has an entry extending to the best part of a page in the *DNB*, but, while some few will continue to turn up his *Annals of Nottingham-shire*, it is unlikely that anyone will bother to read any more his *Ireton*, or his *What is Life?* *and other poems* (1820) or even his *Carnival of Death* (1820). Why did the well-to-do wine-merchant of Friary Lane bother to write them? It is a question that one asks of the authors of hundreds of poems written in those years. The Howitts, man and wife, produced their fair share. The pheno-menon is no less interesting than their persistent radicalism and no more important. All over England these pigmies of Parnassus were turning out their parish-magazine poems. It is as if the human race, or at any rate the English part of it, must forever be covering sheets of paper with small black hieroglyphics in order somehow to obscure the awful emptiness that lies before them. One needs to affirm one's essence, as Matthew Arnold used to say when he was trying to account for the eccentricities of the Nonconfor-mists. A century after the time when the Baileys and the Howitts and the rest were turning out their poems, their twentieth-century counterparts were turning out 'novels'. The difference was not much more than a difference between two forms of literary twaddling. There was no difference at all between their respective shares of literary talent. Their claims to be remembered are similarly calculable by subtraction. Take away the 'poems' and the 'novels' and reckon up their contributions to the happiness or even the minimal well-being of their fellow men and women and where do they stand?

Thomas Bailey stands high, and his eminence is beyond all description in political or party terms. Above all else he deserves the title of 'The Friend of Man', a title much coveted in the previous century and commonly deserved by many a man of business in the years between Peterloo and Victoria. Out at Bas-ford where he lived in 'a fine Old English Mansion, embowered in stately foliage', he played the part of a latter-day type of the country gentleman. He was no Sir Roger de Coverley but a man of business who had made money in the silk-hosiery trade and who continued to prosper at his wine-vaults in Friar Lane. His house at Basford was, and is, a stone-fronted building bearing the date 1739. It has a good pillared gateway with some fine local wrought-iron and a handsomely panelled hallway. It has been surmised that the front of the mansion originally consisted of a covered court above which the upper storeys were borne on stone pillars, so that the house possessed a handsome drive-in for carriages. Here Thomas Bailey wrote his *Annals* and his miscellaneous prose and poetry, and here also Philip composed much of *Festus*, Basford House was, and still is, a country house set down on the edge of the town. The gardens once extended to Basford Church and contained pools where goldfish swam, not to mention a willow which is said to have sprung from the one that grew on Napoleon's tomb at St Helena. The whole place, long ruined by the encroachment of the Midland Railway Company, must once have served as a suitable provenance for *Festus* with its scene-directions, 'Wood and Water', 'Colonnade and Lawn', and many another setting that would not be alien to suburbia. The neighbouring town of Nottingham may well have served for such scenes as 'A Country Town—Market Place—Noon'. When *Festus* was written Nottingham Market Place, that spacious area of more than five acres, and the largest in England, was unencumbered by the stone fitments that have caused local folk to christen it 'Slab Square'. Its Georgian Exchange looked down with the serene and handsome dignity which still survives in local memory despite its pompous replacement by the modern 'Council-House'.

Thomas Bailey made Basford House the headquarters of his latterday squiredom. As Malcolm Thomis has said, 'It is in his capacity of friend and adviser to the working-classes of Nottingham that Thomas Bailey did his more remarkable writing'. He had been asked in 1833 by the local framework-knitters to assist them in drawing up a petition to Parliament for the regulation of their trade. The men of the trade had been trying to secure parliamentary regulation for their trade for years. It was the lowering of standards, and especially the production of 'cut-ups', (stockings cut from the woven piece instead of shaped to the leg on the frame), rather than simply the introduction of machinery, that had let to the prevalence of machine-breaking. Thomas Bailey was not content with simply stating the workmen's case for regulation. He produced a document which stated working-class complaints in the context of capitalist industry, forecast the advent of class-war and argued cogently for the workers' side of the struggle. Malcolm Thomis, who characterises Bailey's statement in these terms, has called this 'an important contemporary contribution to what was later to become the great standard of living controversy'. Bailey considered that the Industrial Revolution had failed to bring any tangible benefits to the great mass of working men whose labour had brought it about. Unlike the doctrinaire economists, he developed the argument for the labourer's right to the whole product, but elaborated a case for the creation of a 'National Labour Fund' created by a 10% tax upon inherited property in order to establish and maintain a fund for retirement pensions at 60 and compensation for injury. 'Bailey's pamphlet was a most eloquent plea for society's excluded and underprivileged members and a bitter castigation of the economic system.' It was prophetic of the welfare-state, and an example of Carlyle's view that the industrial problem must be solved by those who lived in it and with it. Nor did he stop short at the larger vision. He worked consistently for immediate issues such as the Artisans' Library and the Mechanics' Institute, the upkeep of highways in the parish and the care of sufferers in the cholera epidemic of 1832. He got together a fine gallery of paintings, and he built up a first-class collection of fossils. Geologist, art-collector, poet, lecturer, patron of public health and highways, there was very little that Thomas Bailey passed by, and all this without assuming a party name, unless he may be said to have called himself a Tory when he outgrew the Whig Radicalism of his young manhood. It is in men like Thomas Bailey that history eludes the categories, escaping through the fingers like water, very clean water.

When he stood as a candidate for Nottingham at the elections of 1830, Thomas Bailey's election address concluded with a scornful denunciation of the political corruption of the times. 'To accomplish the object so near to my heart,' he said, 'I ask but the suffrage of honourable and independent-minded electors—of honest and unbought voters', adding that he entertained no doubt of there being a sufficient number of them among the electors of Nottingham to place him in the situation to which he aspired. For the rest, he declined to buy a single one of the tribe, nor would he do so even if he possessed the wealth of the Indies. Only half of his address has survived, but needless to say Thomas Bailey stood for reforms of all kinds, including liberty of the press and the extinction of slavery in the British Colonies. He offered the electorate the slogan:

Free trade for ever. Reform in the Laws.
In Nottingham then shall prosperity reign.

'For ever' apparently extended more than some eight years for in 1838 we find him making a stout speech against free-trade on the town council. In fact, it was his conversion to protectionism by that time which caused him henceforth to call himself a Tory. He was always open to persuasion by facts, and he had come to the conclusion that free-trade was placing the country at the mercy of 'the autocrat of all the Russias'. Somewhat similarly he had been put against the Radicalism of Cobbett by the spectacle of that self-styled champion of the people complaining of the low profits of the lecture he gave in Nottingham in 1831. After he acquired *The Nottingham Mercury* in 1845, its circulation declined to the point of extinction largely as a result of his refusal to go in for extreme courses or policies. He was not only opposed to corruption in parliamentary government but town government too. He was liable to concern himself with the beam that was in Nottingham's eye as well as the beam that was in Westminster's. It is not really surprising that he was never elected a Member of Parliament, and that his newspaper failed. It is pleasant to discover among his papers a letter from an old Chartist which reveals the fact that there were some who saw Thomas Bailey for what he was. 'Sir,' the old witness ends his letter, 'in conclusion I have watched your progress for years and remember your struggle against Whiggery, now nearly twenty years since, and my experience dictates to me that you are no Tory. If I mistake not, you are a man of the People and live for the People. You have thrown party to the winds, resolved to do justice and love mercy. Pursue, then, your noble career, and all who are truly good will aid and assist you. Most respectfully yours, But an uncompromising

Chartist.' He once wrote of the working classes in a letter to his son, Philip: 'I know them well and understand them well—no man better—I walk with them and talk with them, and argue and discuss these subjects with them every day of my life'. Such was Thomas Bailey of Nottingham. Such men are the salt of the earth.

When Philip James Bailey had completed his original draft of *Festus* he dedicated it to his father in words that were a great deal more than a filial formality. His father, he said, had made him 'the sum of man in all his generous aims and powers'. To earn his father's love was more to him than to earn immortality or to string his harp with golden strings. While composing the poem he passed on the sheets to his father as they were written, and that inveterate poetiser maintained a keen interest in the work as it grew, tempered by some apprehension. 'Don't forget in the employment of your time,' Thomas Bailey wrote, 'that law and not poetry is to be the business of your future life'. Philip managed to forget it almost completely for a great part of the time. Like Wordsworth before him, like Browning and Tennyson his contemporaries, he was to be the typical full-time poet of the nineteenth century. As Arthur John Lawrence said to the author of *Sons and Lovers* when he heard that his son had been paid fifty pounds for it, 'Fifty pahnds! Tha's niver done a day's hard work in thy life'. Certainly Philip Bailey, no more than Browning and Tennyson and Wordsworth, ever did anything but write poetry. That, after all was the guarantee that it would be poetry. 'It seems odd to me when you ask if I have done anything more to my poem,' he told his father. 'I certainly add to it as the day does to the year. I flatter myself, too, that I keep improving it. Its magic haunts my dreams by night; it's all my thoughts by day. It is my beautiful, my heart's delight . . . I feel as if I shall never do anything else . . . ' And over a life-time of eighty-six years, he never did.

CHAPTER 9

Festus

PHILIP BAILEY was born two years before Peterloo. He reached his majority in the year of Victoria's accession. He was to outlive both the Queen and the century.

Festus belongs to the lean years of the 'thirties, but it was very far from being a lean poem. It began as a poem of just over 8,000 lines, and in the poet's lifetime it grew to nearly 40,000. It grew because he incorporated in it large portions of other, less successful works. Thus, as the years went on, he found a way of defeating the public which rejected everything he wrote after *Festus*, and nobody complained. The fortunes of *Festus*, elongating and fattening himself, are the fortunes of poetry in the Victorian Age, almost those of literature itself. We ignore it at our peril.

The trouble with *Festus* is that the world has rather too readily assumed that it belongs to the Faust tradition. The error is both serious and light-hearted. Elizabeth Barrett, a fervid admirer, thought it a misfortune that Festus was 'formed upon Goethe's, and has thus no originality of design'. Nonetheless she wrote of its pinnacles of grandeur and profundities of madness. Parts, she thought, were 'as bad and weak as is well possible to conceive of. But what poet-stuff remains'. As for the comic view, it is best expressed in the lines denominating Bailey, satirical, surly,

> Who studied the language of Goethe too soon,
> And sang himself hoarse to the stars very early
> And cracked a weak voice with too lofty a tune . . .

While all the time Bailey himself had said that the scheme of the poem was 'almost the reverse of that of the Devil and Doctor Faustus'. The only reason for reading, or taking any particular

notice of Bailey's *Festus* today is that he had departed from the
Faust story—liberated himself from it, one might say. Here is a
young man (only a year or two beyond twenty) living in the industrial Midlands in the reign of King William the Fourth, who had
rejected almost contemptuously the legend that modern man had
sold himself to the Devil and shut himself forever out of Heaven.
He had, instead, taken the position of Pierre Cuppé in his heretical
book, *Le Ciel ouvert à tous* (Heaven open to everyone) though it is
unlikely that he had ever heard of it. The whole point of *Festus* is
that of universal salvation. As Lucifer is made to say:

> Sin, the dead branch upon the tree of Life,
> Shall be cut off for ever; and all souls
> Concluded in God's boundless amnesty . . .

It would seem he had better have said 'included' rather than 'concluded'. Anyway, the point is clear. Bailey is concerned to pro-
claim the doctrine of Universalism, or the belief that all men will
be saved. A comforting belief, no doubt, but fatal to tragedy.
Bailey, indeed, is an early example of what has been called 'the
Death of Tragedy'. If we are all going to Heaven, where is there
room for ultimate tragedy?

The impossibility of Tragedy in Bailey's scheme of things is
enunciated by God himself in the opening scene of the poem,
when the Almighty tells Lucifer:

> Upon his soul
> Thou hast no power. All souls are mine for aye.

Lucifer thanks God for giving him Festus. He seems to be saying
'Thank you for nothing'. God's gift of Festus is like the gift of
a mouse to a kitten. 'He is thine to temp,' he says. The emptiness,
the triviality, of such a gift becomes clear in the following pages,
for no one has ever been able to say what fun Lucifer gets out of
it. The reader waits, even hopes, for the usual Faust-fun of sensual
temptations, a trip to the Venusberg at the very least, and there is
nothing. It was always said that the Devil gets the best tunes—in
Milton and even in Gounod—but in Bailey he gets nothing but a
lot of rather arid discussion. Who would be Bailey's Lucifer, or

even his Mephistopheles? Robbed of tragedy, the poem loses its
force as drama. 'As a drama *Festus* collapses in the opening scene,'
Robert Birley wrote. It was to be expected from the theology or
philosophy. It was also to have been anticipated from the provenance of Philip Bailey, perhaps even from his paternity. What
else was to be expected of 'Phil' Bailey, the boy from Basford who
went to Nottingham High School, a familiar figure in the streets
of Nottingham? Was it really to be expected that anyone but one
of his own characters should have said to him:

> Thy talk is the sweet extract of all speech
> And holds mine ear in blissful slavery?

True, Keats' father kept a livery-stable, and even Shakespeare is
said to have delivered a boyhood oration over a bull-calf pole-
axed by his father. And we all know that the wind of genius
bloweth where it listeth. It is when we come upon Philip Bailey's
milk-and-water Liberalism, close on the heels of his universal
salvationism, that one knows—to use a term employed by Robert
Birley—'exactly with whom one is dealing'. That long catalogue
of benefits which Festus asks of God in the prayer of nearly 250
lines which he delivers in the Market Place of the Country Town
(obviously Nottingham Market Place on a busy Saturday morning)
what are they but the Whig-Liberal benefits of peace, ecumenical
religion, fair rewards for labour and for curates vis-à-vis bishops.
Only in *Festus* is it that we suspect the epic characters of sub-
scribing to *The New Statesman*.

Bailey lived nearly as long as Fontenelle, of whom it has been
said that he lived long enough for his age to catch up with him.
Certainly, when Bailey died at the beginning of the reign of
Edward VII, the prayer of Festus in the Market Place, whether of
Nottingham or another smart Edwardian town, falls into place, and
we hear the familiar tones of Lloyd George intoning of England's
spendid future at a Bethesda chapel. In 1839 when *Festus* first
came out it must have seemed greatly ahead of its time, which
gives it its claim to significance in the story of England from
Peterloo to Victoria. Already we hear some of the characteristic
utterances of Victorian poetry presaged.

The bells of time are ringing changes fast.
Grant, Lord, that each fresh peal may usher in
An era of advancement.

Tennyson, who in 1846 was expressing great admiration for 'that now forgotten poem, Bailey's *Festus*,' (it had been out only seven years and was in a second edition) declaring that it contained 'many grand things—grander than anything he himself had written,' was to join in the chorus in his *In Memoriam*, with its CVI canto:

Ring out, wild bells, to the wild sky,

and its welcome to the true, the nobler modes of life, the thousand years of peace, the larger heart, the kindlier hand, indeed all the things that Thomas Bailey had fought for. If his father had written *Festus*, it was the prayer of Festus in Nottingham Market Place that he would have been proudest of. We can well imagine his pleasure when he received those eight or ten sheets from his son's pen. 'If I had to compile an anthology to illustrate the political and social thought of the Victorian era I should include the whole prayer,' Robert Birley said. 'As we read it we recognise that here, in a primitive form, are a good many of the ideas of our own day, even some of those which we believe our own century may claim credit for.' Of these he cites peace, the universal people of the world growing more great and happy every day, mightier, wiser, humbler towards God, the mingling of all ranks, all classes, callings, states of life, like 'sister trees, and so from one stem flourish . . . ' In a poem published in the year of Queen Victoria's accession, and written in the last years of William IV, Bailey is a true Victorian rejoicing in Progress, and well-pleased with his own age:

This time is equal to all time that's past
Of like extent, nor needs to hide its face
Before the future . . .

The bells of time are ringing changes fast.
Grant, Lord! that each fresh peal may usher in

> An era of Advancement, that each change
> Prove an effectual, lasting, happy gain.
> And we beseech Thee, overrule, Oh God!
> All civil contests to the good of all;
> All party and religious difference
> To honourable ends . . .

One of the gains he welcomes is 'mechanic aids to toil' obviating the thousand wants of life, lightening human labour, affording more room to men's minds, leaving the poor 'some time for self-improvement . . . ' The son of Thomas Bailey, patron of the Nottingham Mechanics' Institution who had been as inveterate a lecturer as Uncle Joseph Finsbury or any member of the Adult Education Movement, was the true son of his father.

In *Festus* there is, too, a premonitory echo of Kipling and the *Recessional*)

> Lord God of armies, let our foes
> Have their swords broken and their cannon burst,

while we 'faithfully and righteously, improve, civilize, christianize the lands we win from savage or from nature . . . ' There is a touch of Milton, and God's especial people, in the ending of this prayer:

> Vouchsafe, kind God! Thy blessing on this isle,
> Specially! May our country ever lead
> The world, for she is worthiest . . .
>   (2nd ed. p. 81)
> Thou, oh God!
> Will aid and hallow conquest, as of old,
> Thine own immediate nation's.

He looks forward to the day when 'all mankind may make one brotherhood,' when 'every race, red, black or white, olive, or tawny-skinned' shall live in peace together beneath the great Prince of Peace! And Philip Bailey was a patriot along with the best of the Victorians. As Festus rides above the earth with Lucifer in his Walpurgis night he sees far below the English on their knees at the feet of Victoria, singing:

England's hope, and England's glory!
Hail Victoria! Princess hail!

On Ascension Day, 1895, when he was in his eightieth year, he lunched with Arthur Christopher Benson,* author of 'Land of Hope and Glory!', but he was in his grave at the Church Cemetery in Nottingham when Elgar set the words to music in a *Pomp and Circumstance* march. Bailey's best patriotic verse in *Festus* comes also in the Walpurgis night ride.

England! my country, great and free!
Heart of the world, I leap to thee!

The passage is an invocation to the sea, within those arms England must live and die. America, too, where *Festus* always enjoyed great popularity, and went into many editions—pirated, of course, —America comes in for what is probably the best aphorism in the poem:

America! half-brother of the world!
With something good and bad of every land.

Some, however, may prefer Lucifer's wish: 'I should like to macadamize the world; the road to Hell wants mending.' (1845, p. 85, 1.3)

The Bailey-Festus syndrome brings us to the opening of the Victorian Age and beyond, containing as it does vivid indications of the spirit of that age, its liberal theology, its optimism, its confidence in the special appointment of the nation by God to the vanguard of civilisation. We are impressed with the sovereignty of a people who have passed beyond politics in the sense that they are neither Whig nor Tory and least of all Radical, who might very well say of itself, as Disraeli said of himself, 'my politics can be expressed in a word—England'. There was a great deal of narcissism about the song of the people whom Festus heard singing around the throne: 'Hail Victoria! Princess hail!' Some would

*See MS note inside cover of 1851 Anniversary Edition, Cambridge Univesitry Library, for Bailey's appearance at lunch that day.

call it 'chauvinism', a word commonly used in the twentieth century without knowledge of its origin or meaning. 'Chauvin' was the name of a Napoleonic veteran in a French play of 1831 called *Cocarde Tricolore,* or the tricoloured cockade. From his gasconading nationalism arose the use of the word 'Chauvinism' for bellicose patriotism, and with typical misapplication of an easy adjective for a quality that has later earned dislike, it gave rise to the word 'chauvinism' for all and every form of national pride. By the second year of Victoria's reign, when Bailey's *Festus* came out, the English were well on the way to the good conceit of themselves which had been steadily growing since the victory of Waterloo. They were the people, as Tennyson was to say,

> whom the roar of Hougoumont
> Left mightiest of all peoples under heaven.

The farm at Hougoumont had seen the bloodiest fighting at Waterloo.

This mighty people, who have sung paeans to themselves at least once in every century since Agincourt, the latest being framed in *Land of Hope and Glory,* has recently been schooled by two great men who left them in no doubt, not of their invincible might but of their unquestioned capacity for adapting themselves to the new century. Jeremy Bentham did for them what the French Revolution and Napoleon had done for France, and Samuel Taylor Coleridge lodged them on a philosophical plane in no way inferior to that prescribed for the Germans by Immanuel Kant.

CHAPTER 10

The Teachers of the Teachers of the 19th Century

THE PHRASE was invented by John Stuart Mill of the two great men when he wrote his celebrated pair of essays on Bentham and Coleridge for the London and Westminster Review in 1838 and 1840. They had both recently died, on the eve of the Victorian Age, having put into circulation the greater part of the important ideas of the thinking men of their time, indeed, Mill held, having brought about 'a revolution in its general modes of thought and investigation'. 1832 is more often remembered for the passing of the Great Reform Bill than for the death of Jeremy Bentham at the ripe old age of 84, but like the lethal years 1821–1824, a decade earlier, it was a bad year for literature which saw the departure not only of Bentham (whom Letters might not have missed) but of Scott and Goethe, a year which eclipsed the gaiety of nations as Dr. Johnson said when Garrick died. Two years later Samuel Taylor Coleridge was finally delivered from that long disease called his life. They were, Bentham and Coleridge, said Mill 'the two great Seminal minds of England in their Age'. They were verily, 'the Teachers of the Teachers'.

Mill overstated the contrast between them, although he did grasp correctly that they were both 'questioners of things established', for, as he said, 'a questioner needs not necessarily be an enemy'. It is when he tells us that Bentham took his stand Outside the Received Opinion, while Coleridge looked at things from Within and endeavoured to see them with the eyes of a believer, that he goes astray. After all it was Bentham who began his first major work with what amounts to an exordium upon the Age. 'The Age we live in is a busy Age; in which knowledge is rapidly advancing towards perfection. In the natural world, in particular, everything teems with discovery and improvement.' Coleridge, on the other hand, can never refrain from scathing comment on the contemporary jargon about 'our enlightened Age' and cries out with pained amusement at the very triumphs that Bentham would rejoice in. A volume, probably Colquhoun's, celebrating the latest inventions, discoveries, public improvements, docks, railways, canals, etc. leads him to exclaim: 'We live under the dynasty of the Understanding, and this is its Golden Age.' Talking of its blessings, 'dare we unpack the bales and cases so marked and look at articles, one by one? Increase of human life are, it is true, with the increase of the means of life, reciprocally cause and effect; and the genius of commerce and manufacture has been the cause of both to a degree that may well excite our wonder. But do the last results justify our expectations likewise?' He finds the subject a painful one and points at the report of medical men concerning the state of the manufacturing poor . . . We are, and long may we continue to be, 'a busy enterprising and commercial nation—at least until we can become something better'. These observations belong to *The Statesman's Manual* which he composed in 1816. In *The Constitution of the Church and State*, which came out a little more than ten years later (in 1829), he wrote a fine paragraph to end the sixth chapter, turning away from the manifold triumphs of technology the fruits of the Understanding or 'the faculty of means to medial ends', in order to ask—what of ultimate ends? 'Where shall I seek for information concerning these? By what name shall I seek for the Historiographer of Reason? Where shall I find the annals of Her recent campaigns? the records of her conquest? In the facts disclosed by the Mendicant Society? In the reports of the increase of crimes? In the proceedings of the Police? Or in the accumulating volumes on the horrors and perils of population?'

Coleridge, in fact, was no quiet observer of his age, content to ask of an ancient or received opinion, 'What is the meaning of it?', rather than (as Bentham would say) 'Is it true?', In fact, if it is a matter of radicalism, even revolution, it is the philosopher of Highgate Hill rather than the sage of Queen's Square Place, who must bear the palm. To take a mere detail of contemporary

10 Nottingham Castle burning during the Reform Bill riots.

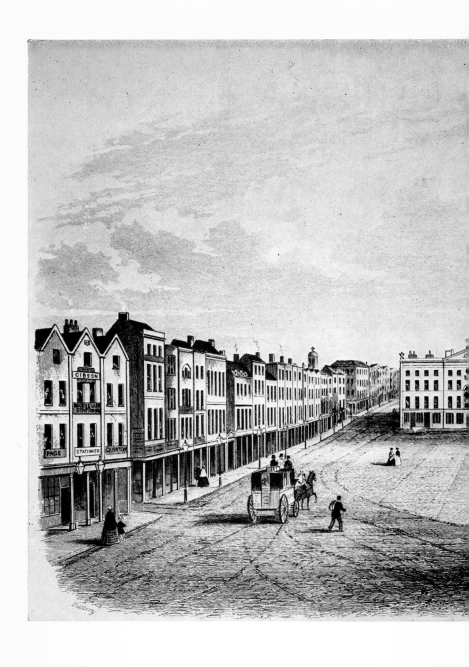

11 Nottingham Market Place in 1855

12 Philip James Bailey, 'Festus Bailey', the Nottingham Poet.

13 William and Mary Hov

politics, Bentham could show himself acquiescent even smug, about a question like the emancipation of women, while Coleridge was prepared to follow up the consequences of his own argument to the end. Macaulay pointed out that Bentham and James Mill would be content that wives and daughters should be represented by the suffrage of their husbands and brothers, a position which conflicted with their adherence to the self-preference principle. Shelley, a greater liberal than Macaulay, inclined to think female suffrage, even in the 1820's, premature. Coleridge was arguing at the time of the Great Reform Bill that if the House of Commons was to be reconstructed on the principle of 'A delegation of men, there was no reason why reform should stop short of universal suffrage; and in that case I am sure that women have as good a right as men'. But then, he had gone deeper into the question than the Utilitarian Radicals and knew full well that the so-called 'Reformers', in appealing to the argument of the greater numbers of voices were destroying 'the sacred principle in politics of a representation of Interests', and were introducing 'the mad and barbarizing scheme of a delegation of individuals'. He was not opposed to a mere extension of the franchise, indeed 'I should be glad to see it greatly extended', but he could not discover 'a ray of principle in the Government plan'. What was the significance of the 'ten-pound Householder'? He called it 'an unmeaning and unjustifiable line of political empiricism'. To a Radical such as Coleridge, i.e. a really, not a merely avowedly, 'Philosophic Radical', it was necessary to go much deeper than any Benthamite went, much nearer to the root of the question, and after all the very term 'Radical' comes from the Latin radix or root. Towards the end of his essay, Mill exclaims 'How much better a Parliamentary Reformer is Coleridge than Lord John Russell. . . . Most of all ought an enlightened Radical or Liberal to rejoice over such a Conservative as Coleridge'. Mill hoped that his essay might do something to show that 'a Tory philosopher cannot be wholly a Tory, but must often be a better Liberal than Liberals themselves'. Indeed when the young men called the 'Coleridgeans', headed by John Sterling and F. D. Maurice began to attend the debating society which Mill and his fellow-Liberals held fortnightly at the Freemason's Tavern in 1825, he at once recognised

D

them 'as a second Liberal or Radical Party, on different grounds from Benthamism and vehemently opposed to it'. This was at least fifteen years before the essay on Coleridge, where he is consistently described as a Tory philosopher, and his philosophy as the 'Germano-Coleridgean', although Mill is looking back from a later date when he was writing his *Autobiography*. This is the principal defect of Mill's essay on Coleridge, a misapprehension which makes that supposedly 'classic' essay dangerously misleading. If 'classic' means authoritative, nothing could be further from the truth. The initial error was that of the age, and might be summed up in the adjuration—'When in doubt, call it German'. The principal critics of the age were indebted rather to the French, whether directly, through the dominance of the 'Enlightenment' or through such Scottish philosophers as David Hume. These last were the natural intellectual progenitors of the Mills, father and son, indeed of the Utilitarians in general, who knew little or no German, although they were aware that the Germans possessed a profound and important secret which it behoved all learned men to know: what another Scot, Thomas Carlyle, called 'the secret of believing by "the reason" what "the understanding" had been obliged to fling out as incredible'. The mockers called this 'High-German Transcendentalism', or (again Carlyle) 'bottled moonshine'. As soon as a man began to use words like '*Vernunft*' (reason) and '*Verstandt*' (understanding), and particularly if he made out that there was a vital difference between them, everything else he said was likewise distrusted, even ridiculed. Now the young Coleridge had lived for some months in Germany, and had learnt the language, and attended learned lectures in the High-German Philosophy. When he came back, and for ever after, he was suspect of the intellectual legerdemain which was always supposed to go with German philosophy, what was called the cant that begins with a 'c' as well as the Kant that begins with a 'k'. The fact that Coleridge had, as he told them, 'toiled out' for himself most of what he found confirmed by Kant, and that he had served his philosophical apprenticeship to the Greeks, and then to the English Neo-Platonists of the 17th century, not to mention the English poets, Shakespeare and Milton, was beyond their belief, let alone their understanding. The great document for his intellectual ancestry is his *Statesman's Manual*, a work known mostly to the inner circle of his disciples, and, calamitously, it would seem not at all to John Stuart Mill. Among all the works cited in the footnotes to the essay on Coleridge, *The Statesman's Manual* is conspicuous by its absence. Without it, what a man says about Coleridge is like 'Hamlet' without the Prince of Denmark.

The fact that *The Statesman's Manual* is among the most abstruse of his work helps to account for its neglect. There is also to be remembered its misleading title. Mill, one suspects, either ignored or passed over it out of the customary disregard of the Utilitarians for anything akin to mysticism. Bentham himself had a favourite expression for all moral speculations to which his own method had not been, perhaps could not be, applied. It was 'vague generalities'. As Mill himself points out in his essay on Bentham, he failed to derive light from other minds. To quote Mill: 'His writings contain few traces of the accurate knowledge of any schools of thinking but his own; and many proofs of his entire conviction that they could teach him nothing worth knowing'. He speaks in his *Deontology* of Socrates and Plato, Mill regrets, 'in terms distressing to his greatest admirers'.* Thus, Mill's master dismissed under the term 'vague generalisations' the whole unanalysed experience of the human race. His severely empirical way of thinking was untempered by imagination, a faculty in which he was deficient. 'The incompleteness of his own mind as a representative of universal human nature' was perhaps, as Mill says, 'his disqualification as a philosopher.' Mill made valiant efforts to break away from his Benthamic ancestry, in other words to be as unlike Bentham as possible, but he never quite managed it. When Carlyle first came upon his work, when Mill was a young man, he is said to have exclaimed 'Another mystic!', but when he read the *Autobiography* fifty years later he could not forbear to call it 'the autobiography of a steam-engine'. Unlikely, we may think,

---

*Metaphysics he said was 'a sprig of logic'. In the *Deontology*, Bentham had spoken of Socrates and Plato talking nonsense under pretence of talking wisdom and morality. 'From the moment of reading that,' Matthew Arnold said, 'I am delivered from the bondage of Bentham! . . . I feel the inadequacy of his mind and ideas for supplying the rule of human society . . . '

to turn out a satisfactory—in the sense of an understanding—
essay on Coleridge.

Nor is Mill's 'Bentham' altogether successful, for he relied
overmuch on his personal memories of the sage in whose house
he had spent a considerable amount of his youth, when Bentham
was an old man. The result is often caricature, the portrait of a
music-hall 'philosopher'—the comic image which even now per-
sists in the mind of posterity. In his anxiety to bring before the
reader a character unrepresentative of universal human nature, he
says things like this:

> He had neither internal experience, nor external: the quiet tenor
> of his life, and his healthiness of mind, conspired to exclude him
> from both. He never knew prosperity and adversity, passion nor
> satiety: he never had even the experiences which sickness gives;
> he lived from childhood to the age of eighty-five in boyish
> health . . . He was a boy to the last.

He is said to have learnt nothing from other ages and other
nations. This of the man who, as a child, used to lag behind his
parents on country walks in order to devour Rapin's *Ancient
History* and as a young man corresponded with Voltaire and
Catherine the Great, Empress of Russia. The fact is that John
Mill, like William Hazlitt, only knew Bentham in old age, long
after he had ceased to interest himself in new acquaintances and
(like most elderly men) had ceased to travel abroad. It is true that
Bentham left other Radicals to face the hustings, and in Hazlitt's
words, confined himself to sticking up a handbill to say that he
(Jeremy Bentham) being of sound mind, was of the opinion that
Sir Samuel Romilly was the most proper person to represent
Westminster. How much he was known in the distant parts of the
world was not merely a matter of 'the plains of Chili and the mines
of Mexico' as Hazlitt put it, but of the Alcalde whom George
Borrow met when he was peddling Bibles in darkest Spain for the
British and Foreign Bible Society. The Alcalde boasted that he
knew sufficient of the English language to read the writings of
'Baintham', but he found it curious that a countryman of 'the
great Baintham' went about selling such an old monkish book as

the Bible. Borrow agreed that Bentham was 'a very remarkable man in his way', but the Alcalde corrected him in his moderation:

'In his way!—in all ways. The most universal genius which the world ever produced—a Solon, a Plato, and a Lope de Vega.'

Borrow agreed as to Solon and Plato, but he thought it was going too far to compare him with Lope de Vega. That, said the Alcalde, simply showed that Borrow knew nothing of his writings.

'Now here am I, a simple Alcalde of Galicia, yet I possess all the writings of Baintham on that shelf, and I study them day and night.'

No doubt the story is an instance of George Borrow's blarney, and it is remarkable that the author of *The Romany Rye* lighted upon the father of Utilitarianism for his purposes. As a teacher, Bentham might have been supposed even more 'remote and ineffectual' than Coleridge, but his lessons to his age were similarly secondhand, passed on by a multitude of disciples, among whom were many of the junior intellegentsia of the early nineteenth century. There is indeed a noticeable resemblance between Bentham and the first generation of Utilitarian Radicals and the members of the Fabian Society under the influence of Sidney and Beatrice Webb in the present century. Both worked indirectly upon their age and country, chiefly through personal conversion of the young.

If Bentham was under-rated in his own time, he has, if anything, been over-rated in our own. This is probably because the twentieth century goes in terror of slighting intellect and under-rating intellect's impact on ordinary men and on the course of history. One of the scholarly persons who helped to over-rate the importance of recluse genius in shaping history was the late G. M. Young. It is a favourite cult of the Romantic, especially in an age and a society where the prizes go to 'men of business'. Coleridge was much given to crying up the glory and the importance of recluse genius in the formative movements of history. Generally being 'recluse' geniuses themselves, it is a way that poets are inclined to take in order to get their own back on men of action. In *The Statesman's Manual* he said that he thought 'it would not be difficult, by an unbroken chain of historic facts, to demonstrate that the most important changes in the commercial relations of the world had their origin in the closets or lonely walks of uninterested theorists . . . in the visions of recluse genius.' G. M. Young is more explicit, in regard to Jeremy Bentham himself. 'It would be hard to find any corner of our public life where the spirit of Bentham is not working to-day,' he wrote in 1936. He also said, in effective language, that it was Bentham who replaced the age of Humbug with the age of Humdrum. He meant that aristocratic governments legislated by guess and by God, but Bentham taught government to legislate on facts—generally facts established by government enquiry. It was long supposed that Bentham initiated the age of the Blue Book, largely on the strength of the great poor-law report of 1833, which resulted in the Poor Law Amendment Act of 1834, which is sometimes called the first example of 'scientific legislation', or an Act of Parliament embodying a principle of social science ('less eligibility') and directed in detail to specific purposes arrived at after the establishment of facts. This is no doubt true, but Benthamite principles were very much the offspring of necessity or common sense, and not greatly related to anyone's philosophic concerns. What Bentham really did was to implant in men's minds the desirability of making the greatest happiness of the greatest number the touchstone of policy and of legislation, together with the concomitant rejection of special privilege for special persons: everyone to count for one, and nobody to count for more than one—the fundamental principle of democracy.* By this means Bentham promoted social justice and happiness.

Bentham was, as Hazlitt said, 'one of those persons who verify the old adage, that "A prophet has most honour out of his own country . . . " His name is little known in England [Hazlitt was writing in 1825], best of all in the plains of Chili and the mines of Mexico. He has offered constitutions for the New World, and legislated for future times.' Perhaps the first man of his time in influence over the minds of men in politics (by the 1840's, as

---

*Bentham laid great stress on the virtues of Equality, but he refused to believe in the value of Liberty. The penultimate paragraph of Chapter IV of the *Principles of Legislation* is the most pungent example of this.

Macaulay asserted, men could say 'we are all Utilitarians now, even if we are not all Benthamites'), he yet took no part in the political arena. He exerted his influence through a whole host of pupils: Romilly, Brougham, Burdett, Place, and a great many bright young men of Cambridge and the University of London, of which he was a founder, and almost the patron-saint. His mummified body presides at meetings of its Council, and indeed one of his quaint plans,—he was as obsessed with ingenious inventions as the White Knight,—was to petrify the bodies of great national figures and stick them up in public places instead of going to the expense of statues in valuable materials like bronze or copper. Bentham was as idiosyncratic as the White Knight, and as benevolent. It was his fond wish that he might re-visit the world every century in order to see how the execution of his plans for the future happiness of mankind had progressed.

Coleridge too worked through disciples, the life-long audience who attended the table-talk at Dr Gilman's house at Highgate. The philosopher-poet in full spate was one of the sights of London. He did not lecture. He did not proceed by question-and-answer. The young sometimes complained that he did not answer their questions. It was not a matter, he would say, of supplying answers. They put questions, he complained, that cannot be answered but by a return to first principles, 'and then they complain of me not conversing but lecturing'. It was the same when he lectured; they complained that he conversed, 'rambled' was the word. It was not surprising, for his purpose was to take them on a personally conducted tour of the universe. 'You are going not indeed in search of the New World', he told them. Nor yet another world that is to come, but in search of the other world that now is. He wished to persuade men 'to consider what they are, and not merely what they do'. His purpose was not to 'change men's minds', but to teach them what they are. Thus they would be 'modified'—a favourite word of this uncommon teacher. He was here poles apart from the sytem-maker. His teaching was the language of a temperament, the moralistic, practical, protestant temperament of a deeply English man. The English genius has always been given to poetry and politics. It refuses to subordinate character to knowledge, works to faith, practice to theory.

Appropriately its greatest philosopher was a poet, indeed a playwright. Its greatest philosopher was a poet, a man who saw men always under a political rather than a cosmological order. Nor is it at all surprising that his greatest disciples in Victorian England were not to be found among 'saints of faith' like Cardinal Newman, but among makers of men, like Thomas Arnold of Rugby, Fighters for the Christian Commonwealth like Frederick Denison Maurice, the founder of Christian Socialism, and even liberal Socialists like John Stuart Mill. His English impatience with any intellectual activity which fails to issue, sooner or later, as power, can be illustrated from every period of his life. He never set aside the motto of *The Watchman*: 'That all may know the Truth, and the Truth may make us free. Knowledge is Power.'

CHAPTER II

The Lays of Coleridge

Coleridge: 'Did you ever hear me preach, Charles?'
Charles Lamb: 'N-n-ever heard you do anything else
              C-C-Coleridge.'

IT WAS John Keats who spoke of 'Coleridge's Lays' in a letter of
1816 the year when the first of the two *Lay Sermons* came out. He
made them sound as if they were songs, which Keats no doubt
thought they ought to have been. He says that he read them, so
we may be sure that he very soon found out that they were not, as
everyone else finds, to his regret, if he plucks up the courage to
tackle them. Coleridge wrote them, as Milton might have said,
with his left hand, which was his only hand when he ceased to
write poetry, when 'abstruse research' had stolen 'from my own
nature all the natural man', when 'that which suits a part' had
infected the whole and almost grown the habit of his soul. How
grey the result could be is shown by page after page of the *Lay
Sermons*. It took a young woman to speak plainly about it. 'I have
been reading a pamphlet by Mr Coleridge, which he calls the
Statesman's Manual, a lay sermon,' wrote Sarah Wedgwood early
in 1817. 'It would quite have killed us if it had come out some
years ago, when we were fighting in his cause against his despisers
and haters. I do think I never did read such stuff . . . such an
affectation of the most sublime and important meaning and so
much no-meaning in reality . . . he has the vilest way of writing
that ever man had.' Another young woman, Harriet Martineau,
who 'enacted the hypocrisy of going to see him in the mode
practised by his worshippers', in 1832, was captured and held by
his glittering eye, as the Wedding Guest was held by his Ancient
Mariner, but a few years later Harriet was to decide that the

glitter had been due to opium rather than inspiration. 'And that transcendental conversation, what nonsense it had been.' Coleridge's philosophical utterances, she concluded, were produced by the same kind of action as Babbage's calculating machine, the chief difference being that 'the latter issues from sound premises, while few will venture to say that the other has any reliable basis at all'. If Coleridge were remembered at all, she thought, it would be neither as a poet nor as a philosopher, but as a warning. It is uncertain whether Miss Martineau tried to read the *Lay Sermons*, and perhaps we should remember that the poet's conversation came to her through her famous ear-trumpet. And even if the *Sermons* were not a success with young women, they were enormously successful with hens. John Russell Lowell tried reading them to his Rhode-Island Reds when they had gone off to lay, and reported that 'the effect was magical. Whether their consciences were touched or they wished to escape the preaching,' he added, 'I know not'.

There were to have been three lay sermons. Only two, addressed respectively to the higher, and to the higher and middle classes, were composed. The third, 'to the labouring classes', and referred to several times in Coleridge's letters in the autumn of 1816, was 'to unvizard our incendiaries', or alternatively 'those wretches [who] are most hateful to me as liberticides', by whom he meant extravagantly the brothers John and Leigh Hunt and William Cobbett. The third sermon was never written, and after all two were enough. He had said his say about demagogues in the second sermon, which was the one chiefly relevant to 'the present discontents' of the post-war years. Hazlitt earned his old friend's reproachful indignation by writing a review-article in *The Examiner* of 8th September, 1816, in advance of publication, an article whose 'crass malevolence' Coleridge was to stigmatise with understandable bitterness, for Hazlitt had failed to distinguish between the style and content of the two sermons, a distinction that Coleridge had striven to make clear from the beginning, and which is all-important to the general reader. 'My first I never dreamt would be understood (except in fragments) by the general reader', he had said; 'but of the second I can scarcely discover any part or passage which would compel any man of common education and information to read it a second time in order to understand it', there being only one recondite passage in the whole work.

And it is true. This second *Lay Sermon* was a pamphlet on 'temporary politics and especially on the commercial and agricultural distresses that followed the Peace . . . ' It was, its author said, the only work 'I had meant to be popular, and which, with the exception of three or four pages, really is so,—the work which of all others was calculated to be useful to the public and advantageous to the author.' When a mind like Coleridge's unbends itself in order to bring its thoughts home to men's business and bosoms men owe to their mentor not merely the commonplace attention of a wakeful mind but the imaginative sympathy of an awakened intellect. Here was no prosy disquisition of a layman affecting the pulpiteering manner of a parson. Here was Wordsworth's 'wonderful man' casting pearls. Within the pages of this essay of some one-hundred and fifty pages,* is to be found nearly all the moral and intellectual wealth that justified J. S. Mill in bracketting Coleridge with Bentham as the twin-teachers of the nineteenth century, 'the two great seminal minds of England in their age'.

In the first place, Coleridge scouts nearly all the run-of-the-mill social and political analysis of his time. After a commonplace complaint about the political empirics who infested Regency England, and more particularly the specious lucubrations of the political economist ('What solemn humbug this modern political economy is! What is there true of the little that is true in their dogmatic books, which is not a simple deduction from the moral and religious *credenda* and *agenda* of any good man, and with which we are not all previously acquainted, and upon which every man of common sense instinctively acted?') he comes at a stride to the trade and business cycles of which historians were not to know very much, and to understand even less, for another century and more. Coleridge's discussion of this kind of phenomena led that proud political economist, Mill, to deplore his writings on political economy as the work of 'an arrant driveller'. After all, what

*The greater part of the contents are reprinted in my *The Political Thought of Samuel Taylor Coleridge* (1938) Pt. III.

else was to be expected from a poet who had strayed outside his province? All the same, the poet's political economy, such as it is, has been authenticated by a century and a half of historical experience, while that of John Stuart Mill now flaps its wings like a dodo. Coleridge in fact was in the van of the early nineteenth century revolt against the cramping confines of Adam Smith's *Wealth of Nations*, with its narrow conception of wealth, its disregard of 'spiritual capital'. Commonwealth had come to usurp the place of commonweal in the minds of statesmen, value had usurped the place of worth, and 'worth' itself had become synonymous with 'money's worth'. Coleridge's revolt against this cheapening of words was commonly expressed in his aphorism: 'I still think that men should be weighed, not counted'. In political economy this gave to his thinking a quite different orientation from that of the orthodox political economists of his time. From Coleridge's 'humanistic economics' were to stem most of the welfare-economics of the following century. Without his teaching in the early years, it is almost inconceivable that the Victorian Age would have had John Ruskin, William Morris, and the great tribunes of spiritualized Socialism.

In the second Lay Sermon, Coleridge was concerned with the problem of strengthening what he calls 'the counter-forces to the *impetus* of trade'. He emphasised constantly that he was not hostile to the spirit of commerce, to which he would attribute 'the largest proportion of our actual freedom, and at least as large a share of our virtues as of our vices'. The statement needs to be emphasised in an age when social critics seem to think that there is something morally indefensible about trade and industry as such. Coleridge was no Luddite bearing malice against some such abstraction as 'the machine', or 'the money-power', or 'predatory capitalism'. What he was chiefly concerned with was 'the overbalance of the commercial spirit in consequence of the absence or weakness of the counter-weights'. What were these 'natural counter-forces'? He enumerates three. First, 'the ancient feeling of rank and ancestry'. Men have come to speak of these as ancient prejudices, no longer respected or even sought for in 'our enlightened age'. However that may be, this reverence for 'anciently in families acted as a counterpoise to the grosser superstitions of wealth'. Secondly, the 'general neglect of all the maturer studies: the long and ominous eclipse of philosophy; the usurpation of that venerable name by physical and psychological empiricism . . .' The pursuit of truth for its own sake, Coleridge held, and the reverence yielded to its professors, had a tendency to calm or to counteract the pursuit of wealth. A counterforce is wanting, he insisted, wherever philosophy is degraded in the estimation of society. The third influence, 'alternatively our spur and our curb', was the influence of religion, and it is to this that he gives primary importance, and lengthy discussion.

The passages which follow afford the finest example of Coleridge's grasp upon the sociology of religion. Much has been achieved by such later thinkers as Max Weber and R. H. Tawney in this field, many of whose conclusions Coleridge anticipated. There are here several illuminating pages of discussion of the (now) well-worn theme of Religion and the rise of Capitalism. It was not for another hundred years and more that T. S. Eliot wrote his *Idea of a Christian Society*, but the whole of it may be found in embryo here, and Eliot's little treatise is perhaps the finest testimony we have to Coleridge's inseminating power as a teacher of the teachers of future generations.

Coleridge was living and writing in an age of multifarious religious enthusiasm, the age of a complex evangelical revival which found expression in Methodism, in the Saints of Clapham, and—by way of reaction—in the Established Church itself, soon to blossom forth into the Oxford Movement. 'The religion of best repute among us', Coleridge held, by which he meant that of the 'plain religionists'—and particularly the Quakers,—those devout men and women held that all the doctrines of Christianity were 'so very transcendent, and so very easy, as to make study or research either vain or needless'. And thus, habitually taking for granted all truths of spiritual import, their religion leaves the understanding vacant and at leisure for a thorough insight into present and temporal interests. That, doubtless, was why the Members of the Society of Friends were in general such shrewd, knowing, wary, well-informed, thrifty and thriving men of business. By the same token, this was also why their religion did so little to counterbalance the commercial spirit. Their Christianity was something learnt *extempore*: something 'poured in on the catechumen all and all at once, as from a shower-bath'. Only religion which demands 'the first fruits of the whole man, his affections no less than his outward acts, his understanding equally with his feelings', will reign in the thoughts of a man and in the powers akin to thought, as well as exercise an admitted influence over his hopes and fears, and through these on his deliberate and individual acts . . . ' This is the basis of Coleridge's insistence upon the vital importance of the intellectual content of religion. Long and learned sermons—such perhaps, as his father, the Rev. John Coleridge of Ottery St Mary habitually delivered, and the frequency and warmth of religious controversies—these were symptomatic of the general state of men's minds, evidence of the direction and the channel in which their thoughts and interests were flowing. It was hardly convincing for a Christian to protest that men wouldn't stand for it. 'He forgets with what delight he himself has listened to a two-hours harangue on a loan or a tax . . .'

'Poor Coleridge,' people said. 'He wanted better bread than could ever be made from flour,' But as Charles Lamb said, 'Poor Coleridge! I will not have such a man called "poor".'

CHAPTER 12

Southey's Colloquies

Southey, Southey,
Cease thy varied song
(Byron)

I⊤ is probable that few have ever heard of them save as the title
of a particularly acidulated review by Macaulay in *The Edinburgh
Review* of January 1830, in which the great Philistine began by
expressing his doubts whether a man of Southey's talents and
acquirements could write two large volumes which should be
wholly destitute of information and amusement, and ended by
assuring the readers of *The Edinburgh* that their country would
best continue in her historic course of progress not by the inter-
meddling of Mr Southey's idol, the omniscient and omnipotent
state, but by government minding its own business, leaving
capital to find its most lucrative course, commodities to find their
fair price, industry and intelligence their natural reward, idleness
and folly their natural punishment. Francis Jeffery, the Editor of
the *Review* wrote to the young Macaulay, 'the more I think, the
less I can conceive where you picked up that style'. The essay on
Milton had made him famous overnight hardly less startlingly
than the opening cantos of *Childe Harold* made for the instantane-
ous fame of Lord Byron. When six years later Macaulay slaughter-
ed Southey's *Colloquies*, the young man of 29 who went for the
ageing lake-poet with a bludgeon was hardly a tyro trying out a
'prentice hand.

The answer to Francis Jeffrey's question was to be found in the
nature of the beast, a compulsive talker with brilliant flashes of
silence, according to Sidney Smith, and already known to his
friends as 'Thomas Babble-tongue Macaulay'. It would have better

become him to have left the *Colloquies* uncollected, as he had wished to leave his essays in review of James Mill and the Utilitarian Philosophy on account not only of their asperity but their lack of respect for an older man whose talents and virtues he had never done justice to. It may be doubted whether Macaulay imagined that, he, or anyone else, ever did any injustice to Robert Southey. After all, the elder poet was a renegade Radical, a diehard Tory, and a bore, and Macaulay's style was perfectly fitted for the perpetration of injustice. Not merely was it a style in which it was impossible to tell the truth, but by its antithetical structure it invited the closing of every sentence with a downright lie. Take for instance the sentence in which he imagines himself to have demolished the dialogue between Southey and Sir Thomas More. This was, in fact, an excellent example of the imaginary conversation as a literary vehicle for the imparting of rational opinion. Macaulay pretends that the participants in this dialogue are really both projections of Robert Southey.

> We now come to the conversations which pass between Mr Southey and Sir Thomas More, or rather between two Southeys, equally eloquent, equally angry, equally unreasonable, and equally given to talking about what they do not understand.

As Matthew Arnold said, (writing of the *Essay on Milton*) 'the unsoundness of the essay does not spring from "its redundance of youthful enthusiasm". It springs from this: that the writer has not for his aim to see and to utter the real truth about his object.' The reader who comes to the essay with the desire to get at the real truth about Milton will not be helped. Macaulay's style, Arnold calls, 'Brilliant, metallic, exterior; making strong points, alternating invective with eulogy wrapping in a robe of rhetoric the thing it represents; not with the soft play of life, following and rendering the thing's very form and pressure. For indeed in rendering things in this fashion, Macaulay's gift did not lie.' In fact Arnold's use of the word 'metallic' is inspired, for Macaulay's style was—as someone was to say before the century was out—one of the finest products of the Industrial Revolution. The fact that one enjoys reading him, indeed admires him, does not acquit him of a certain 'barbarian' quality of his mind and art.

Poor Southey, then, might be said to have fallen, if not among thieves, certainly among Philistines. What he was concerned with in his *Colloquies* was to furnish his age and society with one more example of the type of book which goes under the general title of 'Past and Present', and of which the greatest example is the book of that title published by Thomas Carlyle some fifteen years later. Whether this kind of book, utterly dependent upon the force of contrast between different ages or states of society placed in apposition, is effective as a vehicle of social criticism depends very much on the author's grasp of historical reality and the tact *d'ordonnance* he shows in the handling of diverse materials. Southey was indeed a historian, having written extensively of South American subjects and the Peninsula War. He had written at least two historical biographies, those of Nelson and John Wesley, which were to keep his name alive. His prose style was lucid and generally pleasing. *Letters from England,* purporting to be written by a visitor from Spain, came out in 1807 and was re-published by the Cresset Press in an excellent edition by Professor Jack Simmons in 1951. This belongs to the critical *genre* which extends from Montesquieu's *Lettres Persanes* to Lowes Dickinson's *Letters of John Chinaman*.

The full title of the Colloquies is 'Sir Thomas More; or Colloquies on the Progress and Prospect of Society', and Macaulay pokes a good deal of fun at the employment of the great author of *Utopia* as a critic of English society in the reign of William IV. As the Poet Laureate sits reading his newspaper in his study at Keswick on an evening in November, 1817, 'an elderly person of very dignified aspect makes his appearance, announces himself as a stranger from a distant country, and apologizes very politely for not having provided himself with letters of introduction'. The Laureate supposes his visitor to be an American who has come to see the Lake District, and welcomes him because, he says, some of his most agreeable guests have been Americans, men whose talents and characters would do honour to any country. Southey receives full-marks from Macaulay for his enlightenment here. But when the visitor's hand turns out to possess neither weight nor substance, the Laureate's hair stands on end, and he perceives a red streak round the visitor's neck. Sir Thomas More reveals his identity, adjuring his host not to tell Mrs Southey in case she is frightened. Thereafter the Laureate and Sir Thomas visit the local beauty-spots and engage in converse on many topics, a number of which are of more than topical interest. To these discussions, Macaulay thought, Southey brought 'two faculties which were never, we believe, vouchsafed in measure so copious to any human being, the faculty of believing without a reason, and the faculty of hating without a provocation'.

What chiefly enraged Macaulay, engaging him in a scornful diatribe against the author, is the fact that Southey, who had the privilege of living 'in the most enlightened generation of the most enlightened people who ever existed', yet showed himself utterly destitute of the power of distinguishing truth from falsehood. It is these very passages which preserve the *Colloquies* for the esteem of generations which know not Thomas Babington Macaulay save as an entertaining writer of narrative history. Born in the opening year of the nineteenth century, and hearing of the Peterloo 'massacre' when he was an undergraduate, he was to become a distinguished servant of the Queen in India, and to end his comparatively short life (he died before he was sixty) one of the Great Victorians. There had never been the slightest doubt in his mind that England was the first country in the world, the most enlightened, the freest, the most civilized. 'I wish I was as cocksure about anything as Macaulay is about everything', Lord Melbourne once said. How, then, could Lord Macaulay fail to be pained and shocked by a man like Robert Southey, who thought that in some important respects his country was going backwards? Moreover, going backwards was exactly what Southey preferred in matters of technology. He leaves no doubt whatever in his reader's mind that he thought England had been a better, a happier, a more civilized country in the reign of King Edward I than she was in the reign of King William IV. And it was all on account of 'the manufacturing system'. In his opinion England had paid a quite disproportionate price in terms of human life for her commercial system.

'This system', he had made his Spanish visitor declare twenty years earlier, 'is the boast of England. Long may she continue to boast it before Spain shall rival her! Yet this is the system which we envy and which we are so desirous to imitate . . . ' Happily, the numerous feast-days and holy-days of Catholic Spain would prevent her from doing so. 'Heaven forfend that the Spaniard should ever be brutalized by such a system, like the Negroes in America and the labouring manufacturers in England! Let us leave to England the boast of supplying all Europe with her wares . . . that of being the white slaves of the rest of the world . . . It is evident that Southey, like Cobbett, had no delusions about white slavery in the early years of the factory system. Fielden's 'The Curse of the Factory System' was not to be published until 1836, with its indictment of 'Lancashire Slavery', but Cobbett had been demanding for twenty years that Wilberforce and the anti-slavery men include the cotton-operatives in their propaganda. To which, according to Cobbett, they retorted: 'But they were not slaves. Say, rather, they were not black; a thing which they might, seeing the preference which was given to that colour, have well regarded as extremely unfortunate . . . ' In a *Letter from England* (Number XXXVIII), Southey devoted himself to the cotton-manufacture at Manchester, and the pernicious effects of the manufacturing-system. 'There is nothing which he hates so bitterly', Macaulay declares without exaggeration, and it is perfectly true that he called it a system more tyrannical than that of the feudal ages, a system of actual servitude which destroys and degrades bodies and minds. Worst of all, Southey would rather lose England's manufacturing superiority to other countries if this was its cost. 'May foreign competitors drive us out of the field', he prayed, thus restoring our national sanity and strength. The extermination of the whole manufacturing population would be a blessing, if the evil could be removed in no other way. Reciting these 'Luddite' sentiments with horror, Macaulay points out that 'Mr Southey does not bring forward a single fact in support of these views'. He did not learn his political creed from bills of mortality of statistical tables, Macaulay gibed. Such standards were too low and vulgar for a mind so imaginative as his.

Mr Southey has found out a way, he tells us, in which the effects of manufacturers and agriculture may be compared. And what is this way? To stand on a hill, to look at a cottage and a

factory, and to see which is the prettier . . . Here is wisdom.
Here are the principles on which nations are to be governed.
Rose-bushes and poor-rates, rather than steam-engines and
independence.

It was Carlyle who retorted upon Macaulay's request for 'facts
and figures'. In the second chapter of *Chartism* (1839), entitled
'Statistics', he exclaimed *With what serene conclusiveness a member of
some Useful-Knowing Society stops your mouth with a figure of arithmetic*!
'A judicious man', Carlyle wished to remind the devotees of
statistical science, 'looks at Statistics, not to get knowledge, but
to save himself from having ignorance foisted on him'. In other
words, he was already saying 'You can prove anything by statistics'. Particularly, in that age, clever men were proving from
Savings-Bank Accounts that the poor were saving money and
therefore were 'better-off'. Carlyle, after the manner of the child
who pointed out that the Emperor who was so proud of his new
clothes was in fact naked, asked the simple question: 'What
constitutes the well-being of a man?' and answered 'Many things;
of which the wages he gets, and the bread he buys with them, are
but one preliminary item'. He went so far as to assert that 'even
with abundance, his discontent, his real misery may be great'. He
had already said that 'quality in wages was perhaps even more
important than . . . quantity'. Indeed, the metaphysics of quality
was very much over-due in the quantitative age of Bentham and
the Utilitarians. It is the test of *quality* that social critics like Robert
Southey, and the Romantic Poets in general, brought to bear.

'How is it', said I, 'that every thing which is connected with
manufactures present such features of unqualified deformity?'
Thus Robert Southey looking down beside Sir Thomas More
upon the scene at Millbeck where the effects of manufactures and
agriculture could be seen and compared. He was prophetic of
another and greater poet who looked out over 'the awful Erewash
Valley', where he had been born, and from which he never could
tear himself away. 'The Country of my Heart', D. H. Lawrence
continued to call it, even while his gorge rose at the sight of that
ruined countryside. He could look back upon a century and more
of spoliation, indeed at the nineteenth century as a whole, and he

wrote in his essay *Nottingham and the Mining Countryside* (which the editor of *Phoenix*, the posthumous papers of D. H. Lawrence, described as 'a blistering indictment of the crass and blind materialism of English industrialism'): 'it was ugliness which really betrayed the spirit of man, in the nineteenth century . . . The real tragedy of England, as I see it, is the tragedy of ugliness. The country is so lovely; the man-made England is so vile.' The Midland landscape in which he grew up was, as he described it, 'a curious cross between industrialism and the old agricultural England of Shakespeare and Milton and Fielding and George Eliot'. The England of Robert Southey still had more of these rural traditions than of industrialism, but what he was inveighing against, to the scornful comments of Macaulay, was an earlier stage of the process of betrayal. That is why it is said that Macaulay's review, like so many reviews, tells us most about the reviewer, and —it may be added—about the age to which Lord Macaulay belongs, the age that was dawning.

CHAPTER 13

Tracts for the Times

They used to drive about the country in gigs, from one parsonage to another, and leave their tracts behind them. They were
not concerned with the flocks—their message was to the
shepherds.

(Augustine Birell)

THE VICTORIAN Age was to be a great age of religious revivals.
When it opened, the Evangelical Movement had already been
flourishing for nearly half a century, and the most famous of all
the religious revivals of the age—the 'Oxford Movement'—was
in its lusty infancy even before the Queen came to the throne. Its
official birth-date was Sunday, 14th July, 1833, when the Rev.
John Keble preached his Assize Sermon from the pulpit of the
University Church in Oxford, a discourse which was published
under the title of 'National Apostacy'. John Henry Newman was
to write of this event in his *Apologia*, 'I have ever considered and
kept the day, as the start of the religious movement of 1833'. The
evangelical movement from which they all sprang is best written
with a small 'e' for it was one of the great generic movements of
the human spirit, as vast and creative as the Reformation or the
Enlightenment. 'We all came out of Gogol's *Overcoat*', the poets
and novelists used to say about the great literary revival of 19th-
century Russia. So it might be said of English religious movements, from Wesley to Newman. They all came out of the revived
religious consciousness of Western man which captured Europe
in the age of the French Revolution by either action or reaction.
It was Lord Morley who summed it up as the rescue of European
religion from the aridity and formalism of the *ancien régime*. 'I

don't know what I should have made of this world', Carlyle once said, 'were it not for the French Revolution'.

That was the point in time when Europe cast her vote not for pleasure, nor even for happiness, but for God. Carlyle called it 'The Everlasting Yea'. Neither he, nor Sir Walter Scott, is generally spoken of as a progenitor of the Oxford Movement (regularly referred to by Carlyle as 'a species of Puseyism'), yet both were. Sir Walter made the old Catholic times interesting. Carlyle established the view that the problem of the age, and its solution, had to be conceived not in terms of politics, but in terms of religion. *Sartor Resartus* came out the year before the Great Reform Bill and was written at least two years before the Assize Sermon. Few books had more influence upon the 19th-century mind, and more especially the minds of the young intellectuals. So greatly have men's minds and tastes changed that it is almost impossible to understand this to-day. The very things that repel people who try to read it to-day,—the manner in particular— that of a preacher at the top of his voice and interlarding his preachings with a pawky humour,— are the things that made for its enormously influential impact in its own time.

Thomas Carlyle was, of course, a product of Scottish Calvinism, and like most young men of his intellectual and religious breeding, he retained the impress of a spiritual puritanism long after he lost his religious faith. He was forever issuing stormy spiritual directives to his countrymen at the top of his voice, and the first of them (expressed in *Sartor*, Chapter IX of the second Book), is the notorious command: 'Close thy Byron; open thy Goethe'. Byron had been dead nearly ten years. Goethe was to die next year. To us it is inconceivable that one should ever replace the other, least of all in England. Carlyle did better than that. He wrote what has been called 'The Gospel of Silence', in fifty volumes, most of which were not only read in England but many of them acted upon. W. Somerset Maugham once said that in his view Carlyle was 'booked for oblivion', but in his own lifetime Carlyle remained very much alive, and even today people are constantly finding out what they have missed by taking that kind of remark too seriously. They found out very soon that they could not do without the dyspeptic Scot with the 'thunder-and-lightning style'. Reading a magnificent essay like 'Signs of the Times', or 'Characteristics', people discover that he wrote in English, and that Walter Bagehot justifiably called him 'our veteran humorist'. Another Great Victorian, Fitzjames Stephen, once described him as 'our great modern poet', quoting the 'toil-worn craftsman' passage in the fourth chapter of Book III of *Sartor*. W. E. Forster, the father of the Education Act of 1870, a Quaker manufacturer who married a daughter of Dr Arnold, described him as 'the highest, or rather the deepest mind of the age'. Forster was a redeemed Plugson of Undershot. Under Carlyle's influence he became known as the 'Squire' of Burley in Wharfedale, a benevolent despot, which is what Carlyle meant by his Captains of Industry. Forster was later known as 'the only mill-owner ever claimed by the working-men as a friend', though many others came under Carlyle's influence.

It was one of the most notable features of the spiritual history of England in the nineteenth century that its leaders and teachers were not for the most part clerks in Holy Orders but members of the Clerisy, which was Coleridge's name for the learned of all denominations, or of none. There never was such an age for what the cynic sometimes calls 'plain-clothes parsons', nor was there ever an age and a society so eager to kiss the rod that chastised it. We sometimes get the impression that English society was a gigantic enlargement of the congregation of the Welsh Baptist Chapel which applauds the preacher who flays them. Anyone who ever heard a Baptist revivalist preach on temperance in a Welsh chapel fifty, sixty years ago, will know at once what is meant. 'Go on—go on!', the congregation would encourage him. 'Give us more!' Mr Wopsle, clerk of the Thames-side parish in *Great Expectations* believed that he would have made his mark in the Church if it was 'thrown open'. It not being 'thrown open', Mr Wopsle went off and played Hamlet in a company of strolling-players, an appropriate culmination of a histrionic career. Mr Wopsle was the lowest species of a genus common enough in Victorian England. There was in those years a widespread movement afoot to take over the Church of England for utilitarian purposes, indeed—as parish clergy often said, and still say—to 'pinch it'. The idea was certainly afoot in the early eighteen-thirties, to convert the Church into a Benthamite institution of public utility. From an article which James Mill contributed to the *Westminster Review* in July, 1833, on *Church Reform* it is possible to envisage what the Utilitarian plan was in considerable detail. Emphasis is laid upon the desirable social effect of assembling families on the Sabbath, clean and decently dressed, not for purely moral homilies but for lectures on science and 'useful knowledge', mainly political science, political economy, and the elements of jurisprudence. Mill was prepared to include social amusements of a mildly cheerful character, some music and dancing, so long as the latter did not 'slide into lasciviousness'. In order to keep such activities within the bounds of decency and decorum, every parish should be required to elect for itself a master or mistress of ceremonies, a kind of *sportz führer*, and every parish should partake of a communal Sabbath-meal resembling the Agapai, or love-feasts, of the early Christians, care being taken again to avoid intoxicating liquors. Within a very few years, James Mill imagined, it would be possible to unlearn the whole Christian tradition and remodel it on natural theism. The immediate effect of this essay, however, was to injure the circulation of the *Westminster Review*.

This was the kind of thing, rather than the suppression of 10 out of 24 Irish bishoprics, that gave rise to the Oxford Movement, for it was not so much concerned with the organisation and property of the Church as with its very existence as a pastoral and teaching body. A great many more people would be concerned by the theft of the Church from the people by a minority of radical utilitarians in order to propagate their dismal science of political economy, than would be stirred to their depths by the diminution of an episcopal body which demanded the loyalty of a people (in Ireland) who regarded it as an alien institution staffed by a heretic clergy. The notion that the Oxford Movement was the springing to arms of a people in defence of their favourite bishops would be absurd at any time. It reminds one of the late Gilbert Keith Chesterton's deadly satire upon the Welsh's supposed attachment to their hierarchy when Disestablishment was threatened early in the present century. A satire addressed to Lord Birkenhead, then F. E. Smith, in the form of a poem beginning:

'Are they clinging to their Crosses, F. E. Smith?'

and ending:

> Talk about the pews and steeples, and the cash
>   that goes therewith
> But the souls of Christian people? Chuck it, Smith!

Leslie Stephen, a Cambridge man, acidly remarked: 'It is this kind of thing that could lead to reference to the singular and slightly absurd phenomenon called the Oxford Movement'.

And yet, in a way, the Church had already been stolen, as Coleridge groaned in 1830, 'I fear that the Church has let the hearts of the common people be stolen from it'. To invigorate and inspire it with its ancient pastoral—indeed social purpose—would have seemed to many despondent souls to be locking the stabledoor when the horse had already been stolen. By the year 1833, he was coming to the conclusion that there was a curse upon it, 'With the curse of prudence, as they miscalled it,— in fact of fear'. This was in part due to the manner in which its clergy was recruited, as the resident gentlemen. While in France, for example, the village curé was often a beneficed peasant, a man who lived very little differently from his flock, rough, sometimes scarcely more educated, but close to the hearts of the common people. Here—and it was Coleridge who wished it to be so—the clergyman was (ideally at least) 'a germ of civilization', so that not the remotest village should lack 'a nucleus round which the capabilities of the place', Coleridge went on, 'may crystallize and brighten'. The clergyman is with his parishioners and among them; he is neither in the cloistered cell nor in the wilderness, but a neighbour and a family-man, whose education and rank admit him to the mansion of the rich landholder, while his duties make him the frequent visitor of the farmhouse and the cottage. Such a parish priest was the Rev. John Coleridge of Ottery St Mary in Devon, a homely figure in the village, and yet capable (like his best-known son) of preaching far above the heads of his flock, sometimes quoting the Hebrew Scriptures so that they marvelled and admired their parson who, they said gave them the very language of the Holy Spirit.

Coleridge, Carlyle, Mill, all laymen, all were preachers of 'Lay

Sermons', and all were—by action or as promotors of reaction—
profound inceptors, if not always preceptors, of the Movement
which bears the name of Oxford. None of the three belonged to
the University in which that movement took its rise as a more or
less formal affair. From that fact arises its truly national character.
It came to permeate England not as an effulgence proceeding from
the Oriel Common Room, but somewhat more effectively as a
shower of tracts delivered problematically at the door of every
rectory in England. Here was, in very deed, opportunity for the
distributive power of the parochial clergy, Coleridge's 'germs', to
exercise itself. For more than thirty years another gospel had been
carried forth in the buff and blue covers of *The Edinburgh Review*.
With *Tracts for the Times* came the counterblast. By 1839 they were
reported by Rivington, who took them over in 1834, as 'selling
faster than they can print them'. They were short, and considering
all things, sharp. The first, written by Newman himself, bore the
flat and wordy title: 'Thoughts on the Ministerial Commission
respectfully addressed to the Clergy'. It declared that the times
were evil and that no one spoke against them. It asked the cogent
question: on what are the clergy to rest their authority when the
State deserts them? It answered: upon nothing else than their
Apostolical descent. To an age and a society fed for long on the
smooth dogmatism of the *Edinburgh*, it must have made a change
of dogmatics, to say the least. It was considerably cheaper, too.
The *Edinburgh* came out at five shillings at first, and the price was
raised to six in 1809. The Tracts, at first printed by private sub-
scription, were distributed free by private effort. When they came
to be sold to the public they sold poorly, but they were saved as a
publishing venture when they came out in volume form. To
imagine the country parsons of rural England poring over the
Tracts in their rectories would be an exercise requiring a good
deal of imagination. For the most part the authors of the Tracts
were preaching to the converted, and only some few, like the
famous Tract 90, are likely to have reached a wide circulation.
The impact of ideas, however, is impossible of quantitative
measurement in publishers' figures, as everyone knows who has
studied the circulation of even a history-making book like
Rousseau's *Contrat Social*.

The Tract was an extremely popular, if frequently equivocal, organ of propaganda in 19th-century England. 'Tracts for the Times' raised the standard of religious propaganda considerably above the level it had attained, and was to maintain, in the hands of the Evangelicals. They may have been 'difficult' and even dull, but they were untainted by the mawkishly sentimental twaddle generally associated with the word 'Tract', since Thackeray's satire in *Vanity Fair* on that sweetly moral tale, 'The Washer-woman of Finchley Common', and Wilkie Collins' portrait of Drusilla Clack in the *Moonstone*. The puerile prose of the Evangeli-cal Movement was always one of its principal weaknesses in attempting to win the respect of an increasingly literate society, just as its poetry was the weak point of the Oxford Movement. The gist of the whole of the Tracts of the Evangelicals, Cobbett decided when he returned from the U.S.A. and found the country inundated with them, was 'to inculcate content in a state of misery', to teach people to starve without making a noise, and to keep the poor, *this* was most important, from cutting the throats of the rich. One particular example he cites is 'The Life of Peter Kennedy who lived on, and *saved* money out of eighteen-pence a week'. In his young days, Cobbett recalled, the parson's Sermon used to be quite sufficient for the morals and religion of a village. 'Now we [c. 1825] had a busy creature or two in every village dancing about with these Tracts for the benefit of the souls of the labourers and their families.' The head and front of the evil, Cobbett always insisted, was a poisonous person of the name of William Wilberforce, a Yorkshireman whose talents, in spite of twenty years cultivation, Cobbett assures us, 'still remained far beneath mediocrity', although he possessed 'an abundant stock of that presumption of which conceit of extraordinary purity was at once the cause and the effect'. Cobbett could write as well as Gibbon when he liked.

Tracts were easy game so long as they remained in the hands of the Saints of Evangelicalism. *Tracts for the Times* however were not on the whole hortatory in purpose, although some may have expected a familiar homily from the title of Tract 18, by E. B. Pusey, 'Thoughts on the Benefits of the System of Fasting en-joined by our Church', a dangerous subject to tackle in a gross-feeding society, as young Coleridge had discovered when he wrote his *Essay on Fasts* in *The Watchman* in 1796 under the epigraph 'Wherefore my Bowels shall sound like an Harp' (Is. xvi. II), thereby losing many subscribers. Pusey's name bore an echo of the tabby-cat and of pusillanimity.* On the other hand a rumour was going around that the Rev. Edward Pusey was in the habit of holding his children's fingers in the candleflame in order to afford them a foretaste of hell-fire, one of the baseless rumours like the story that he sacrificed a living lamb every Friday, which he solemnly repudiated by declaring that he did not know how to kill a lamb. No, *Tracts for the Times* were neither sentimental nor sensational. They were not even, as a rule, controversial. They were scholarly, sometimes somewhat ponderously so, which was a change for the better after the consciously unintellectual, even anti-intellectual, character of the Evangelical Movement, in the tradition of the Puritan exegesists whom Hooker had rebuffed long before for confusing piety with 'rawness' of wit. The tone of the Tracts was that of Thomas Arnold's favourite amalgam of 'the Scholar and the Gentleman'. They were reluctant to engage in polemics. Rather, like Coleridge, the great apologist from whom they (and especially Dr Arnold) learnt so much, they were ever careful in the disclosal of opinion 'to consider the character of those to whom we address ourselves, their situations, and probable degree of knowledge'. Even as a young Radical Coleridge advised men to be 'bold in the avowal of political truth among those only whose minds are susceptible of reasoning, and never to the multitude . . . ' Tract 80 *On Reserve in communicating Religious Knowledge*, by Isaac Williams, was thought by Sir Leslie Stephen to be in danger of sliding into 'an apology for lying', such was its confused thinking and writing. Stephen was a renegade son of the Clapham Sect with a keen nose for anything susceptible of being suspected of the casuistry of Rome. Dean Church, anxious as he was to speak up for Tract 80, nevertheless thought its publication very unfortunate and untimely, since it might seem to confirm the suspicion that the Tractarians were slippery customers, like the Jesuits. Is it possible that Tract 80 was mistaken by Charles

*P. D. Whitting used to tell his boys at St Paul's, that his 'anima' or soul would call to a cat 'Pusey-pusey-pusey'. Such an anima might be called 'pusillanimous'.

Kingsley for Tract 90 when he launched his notorious attack on Newman in *Macmillan's Magazine* at Christmas, 1863? To an Evangelical it was like a red rag to a bull. Its title was *Remarks on Certain Passages in the Thirty-Nine Articles*, and its object was 'merely to show that, while the Prayer Book is acknowledged on all hands to be of Catholic origin, our Articles also, the offspring of an un-catholic age, are, through God's good providence, to say the least, not uncatholic, and may be subscribed to by those who aim at being Catholic in heart and doctrine'. This conclusion was reached by a detailed examination of the Articles, word by word, sentence by sentence. No one with the slightest pretentions to scholarship, or even literacy, could get away from it. 'This means Rome', people said. They had been raring to say that of Oxford and its queer ways for long enough. The sensation produced by Tract 90, and especially in Oxford, was enormous. Protestant opinion was electrified. Hitherto Tractarianism had laid hold of men of intellectual quality, of warm imagination, of devout nature. Now it seized upon the 'typical Englishman', that mythical but none-the-less important person whom Walter Bagehot called 'the bald-headed man at the back of the omnibus'.

CHAPTER 14

Saints and Dandies

FOR ALL William Cobbett's abuse of William Wilberforce, the latter's best-selling book, *A Practical View of Christianity* (1797), had already taken the field and was not to be dislodged even by Tract XC. Indeed, Newman himself had begun life as an Evangelical, and if one spells the term with a small 'e' he was one all his life. That is the historical significance of Evangelicalism, even with the capital E: it was the matrix of a personal concern, in the deepest sense of the word, for religious belief. To the disciples of Wilberforce, as to the disciples of Wesley, (indeed, even more so) religion was not a matter of intellectually conceived or accepted formularies but of the conversion of the whole man to God's truth. Conversion was the alpha and the omega of the matter. That was what 'practical' Christianity meant. Religious faith thus achieved, and thus held, could not but 'reign' in the mind and soul and faculties. 'It is not enough that we have once swallowed these truths', as the young S. T. Coleridge once said of his own 'practical faith' in the doctrine he was upholding at the moment (it happened to be that of philosophical necessity)—'we must feed upon them as insects on a leaf, till the whole heart be coloured by their qualities and show its food in even the minutest fibre'. This meant living one's religion. Nothing could be more properly or strictly called 'practical'. It was not a matter of what Stevie Smith's cat called 'rushing about doing good', though it was often that too, and some times tiresomely so. Rather it was a matter of living under a self-imposed discipline every moment of one's life. It meant 'keeping an eye on' oneself, and generally keeping a diary of one's days, a practice which might lend itself to hilarious comment by the impious, as Hurrell Froude's dairy did when Lytton Strachey came upon it.

Sept. 29, 1826.

I cannot say much for myself today. I did not read the Psalms and Second Lesson after breakfast, which I had neglected to do before, though I had plenty of time on my hands . . .

Looked with greediness to see if there was a goose on the table for dinner . . .

Such gamesomeness is not a criticism of the Evangelical discipline, only of the unbecoming levity of Lytton Strachey in picking out examples of it in a young man of 23.

Hurrell Froude has been called Newman's *alter ego*, but Newman was never really a man. W. G. Ward, after nearly twenty years of misunderstandings and estrangement from the great leader, told of a dream he had once had of sitting next to a veiled lady at a dinner party and being fascinated and charmed by her conversation to an extent he told her that he had never experienced since he had talked with John Henry Newman at Oxford. The lady, Ward said, replied 'I am John Henry Newman', and raising her veil showed the well-known face. 'Robust and ruddy sons of the Church', Tom Mozley said, 'looked on him with condescending pity as a poor fellow . . . ' He seemed hardly made for this world. Compared with the 'Saints' of the Clapham Sect, Newman was evidently the genuine article. Of him alone, in all his strength and weakness, is it perhaps possible to employ the word saint without quotation-marks. Moreover, he could write almost as well as the super-manly Cobbett. That was a great asset, for the Evangelicals had never been any great shakes when they took pen in hand. It was one of the great attractions of the Oxford Movement that its leaders—when they kept away from poetry—appealed immensely to the aesthetic sense. A man could feel that his religion spoke, and wrote, the language of gentlemen. Indeed the Oxford Movement may be said to have brought religion in England back to the great prose tradition which it seemed to have deserted since Hooker and the Caroline divines. She was back with the 'Beauty of Holiness'. The communion table ceased to be a depository for hats and the font a receptacle for umbrellas. New standards of dignity, reverence and solemnity began to overtake the parish church.

14 William Corder wearing the
'Corder Casque'.

15 Regent Circus, 1851

16 Victoria and Albert on their wedding morning.

There was loss as well as gain in all this, as they discovered at Mellstock when parson Maybole replaced Mr Grinham. Almost the first thing he did was 'to tell the young chaps that they were not on no account to put their hats in the christening font during service. Then 'twas this, and then 'twas that', said Mr Penny, the cobbler . . . 'Now 'tis to turn us out of the quire neck and crop', Tranter Reuben said. 'It must be owned he's not all there', Mrs Penny remarked, overhearing the talk from within doors, 'far below poor Mr Grinham'. ''Tis only for want of knowing better, poor gentleman', said the tranter. 'His meaning's good enough'. Your parson came by fate, as he went on to say, like pitch halfpenny, and no choosing, and it so happened that Mellstock had now a parson who preferred organs to quires. As Mr Maybole said when the quire waited on him at the parsonage about the proposed change: 'I see that violins are good, and that an organ is good; and when we introduce the organ, it will not be that fiddles were bad, but that an organ was better. That you'll clearly understand, Dewy?' 'I will; and thank you very much for such feelings, sir'. Thomas Hardy was born in 1840, and the story told in *Under the Greenwood Tree* may be reckoned as belonging to the years 1835–6. Hardy was recalling the impact of the Oxford Movement in a village not over-far from the University (Christminster in *Jude*) ten years or more after the event. When he wrote the story his father (the model for Tranter Reuben) had ceased to play his fiddle in the parish church for some years, and the choir up in the gallery had given place to the organist down in the chancel. In terms of social loss and gain, the change was to be accounted to the debit side of the Oxford Movement's account.

Did they know anything of the dangers of Romanism at Mellstock? Was the Rev. Mr Maybole a Ritualist, and was the organ suspect as the thin end of the Papistical wedge? Wandering into St Giles', Sandiacre, on the borders of Derbyshire and Nottinghamshire, on a Saturday afternoon, half a century ago, one might encounter old suspicions still alive in the breast of the aged man cleaning the Communion-rail. 'I cannot believe', the old man sighed, sniffing the ghostly air of incense and casting a derogatory glance at the daffodils in the chancel where the ruby lamp told of a reserved sacrament, 'I cannot believe that this was the religion

E

our fathers died for . . . ' Nor was it. The sophisticated decoration of the Anglo-Catholic parish-church of the Puseyite tradition is generally as alien to the naive, not to say crude, decoration of the medieval parish-church as a petrol-engine is to a tumbrel. Perhaps that helps to account for the Dorsetshire peasant's habit of calling Puseyites 'Pugicides'.

Newman's Tract 90 sounded the alarm. Through the eighteen-thirties the Oxford Movement had gone on advancing with, so it seemed, irresistible force, and (as G. M. Young put it) 'the farther it went, the more certain appeared its ultimate objective, and with the publication of Tract XC it seemed to have unmasked itself'. Newman's Tract showed that the Articles of the Church of England, 'were more susceptible of a Catholic than a Protestant meaning', or, as Macaulay phrased it, that 'a man might hold the worst doctrines of the Church of Rome and the best benefice in the Church of England'. So the Tractarians were denounced as Romanists without the courage of their convictions. The chickens of Catholic Emancipation, people could and did declare, were coming home to roost, and after Newman's secession to Rome in 1845, followed by some of the best second-class brains in the Church of England, the country entered into a period of anti-Roman hysteria. The restoration of the Romish hierarchy in England five years later, was accompanied by the raising of the Archbishop of Westminster, Nicholas Patrick Stephen Wiseman, to the College of Cardinals, and his Eminence's pastoral letter ('given out of the Appian Gate'—a mistake for Flaminian) announcing that 'Catholic England had been restored to its orbit in the ecclesiastical firmament'. This was at once denounced by English Protestants as 'Papal Aggression'. The Prime Minister, Lord John Russell, issued a letter to the Bishop of Durham, denouncing the Roman move as the natural consequence of 'Puseyism'—or, as he said, 'a danger within the gates'. *Punch* published a cartoon of Lord John chalking 'NO POPERY' on Cardinal Wiseman's front-door and running away. The Prime Minister's protest was hardly more worth-while, or more dignified, than that.

In Victorian England these things were ominously exciting for it was a society which thrived on ecclesiastical politics. Liturgical science, (the late G. M. Young said) became a passion with the younger clergy. Church building and restoration were accompanied by a sometimes ludicrous preoccupation with symbolism. The cut of a clergyman's vestment became almost as important as the 'lie' of a waistcoat or a cravat had been to Beau Brummel, and Dickens could say without undue exaggeration that the High Churchman of 1850 was the dandy of 1820 in another form. It was not very long since Coleridge, an expert in the production of Lay Sermons, had been regretting the decline in the standard of sermons in general. He had scarcely ceased to complain before the Victorians restored the sermon to all, and more than all its old popularity as the vehicle of religious truth. Parents required their children to repeat to them the heads of the Sermon after morning-service, an exercise which accustomed the young to orderly argument, a quality which has never again been a noticeable feature of popular political debate. Parents and children, rich and poor, great and small, found solace and satisfaction in hearty hymn-singing. The popular congregational hymn supplied the living poetry of the people. Not Tract 90 but *Abide with me* was John Henry Newman's authentic message to his countrymen. It owed more to the Rev. John Dykes's dreary tune than to the poetry of the author of *The Dream of Gerontius*. Not *The Lyrical Ballads,* still less Gray's *Elegy,* it has been shrewdly said could compete for the people's poetic favour with popular hymns like Toplady's *Rock of Ages,* or Charles Wesley's *Jesu, Lover of my Soul,* or Isaac Watts' *When I survey the Wondrous Cross,* while the latter's *O God our help in ages past* was to be rivalled only by Arthur Christopher Benson's *Land of Hope and Glory* as a national anthem on occasions of national solemnity. In every case a maundering or a martial tune mattered more than the 'poetry'. While crowds waited for the speaker to arrive for a political meeting, or the women waited for news at the pit-head after a colliery disaster, or while men, women and children hoped and prayed for the lifeboats to arrive on the decks of the *Titanic* going down in mid-ocean, it was the fifth-rate litanies of the Victorian religious revivals that held the hearts of the people. Army Regulations bracketed together 'hymns and dirty songs' as the forbidden accompaniments of route-marches.

To a society which loved aristocracy and habitually made obeisance rather on passing the Bank of England than St Paul's Cathedral, the Oxford Movement with its well-bred clergy and its breeding-grounds at the Woodard Schools enjoyed a social cachet which gave rise to the kind of sardonic observation that Coleridge expressed when he referred to Mrs Christopher Wordsworth (Priscilla Lloyd that was) as being ready to 'take up the Cross of the Lord, and mortify the pomps and vanities of the world' on £2,000 a year. 'Few family histories,' Geoffrey Faber wrote, 'can show a more consistent record of material advancement' than that of E. B. Pusey. John Henry Newman, who may have had Jewish blood, had a good head for business, was the son of a banker and born in Old Broad Street, hard by the Bank of England, and his mother was the daughter of a Huguenot draper of pure French descent. Cardinal Manning's father, we are hardly surprised to learn, was actually a Governor of the Bank of England as well as a rich West Indian merchant. The 'Saints' of Clapham, indeed the upper crust of the Evangelicals in general, were a well-heeled crowd who lived plainly and sent their sons to public schools. Where a well-to-do family dissented too far from the formularies of the Established Church they rarely suffered serious restrictions in the matter of schools and universities. They could, and often they did, found their own. Lytton Strachey expatiated on what he called the 'fatal' consequences of an Oxford education for Newman and the historical consequences that would have followed if Mr Newman (post-chaise at the door) had taken the road for the other University on that December morning in 1816. All that can be said about that was said by Geoffrey Faber nearly 40 years ago when he wrote: 'there would have been a Cambridge Movement of some kind or another . . . ' Edward Fitzgerald at Ely Cathedral in 1843 visiting Dr Peacock, the Dean, appreciated being entertained with 'High Church honours of all sorts from chanted Litanies to still Champagne'. It is true that Ely is not Cambridge, but the two Universities were, and are, more like each other, than either is like anything else on earth.

Fitzgerald belonged to the Cambridge Trinity as Newman belonged to the Trinity of Oxford, 'a most gentlemanlike College', as Dr Nicholas, Headmaster of Newman's old school at Ealing said when he heard that his pupil was entered there. He might have said the same of the 'Movement'. In the then state of English society, however, to be 'gentlemanlike' did not disqualify either a person or an institution from social repute, or even from representative Englishness of character. This being so, there is still something remarkable in the way that typical Englishmen could see the women of their families, and even the more imaginative men go in for prayer and fasting, candles and confession, without undue alarm. Of course they knew where to draw the line, and Mr Gladstone showed unspeakable unkindness towards his youngest sister, Helen, who 'went over' to Rome in the Newman secession; she had always been 'peculiar' he, and the family, said. In a man, 'unEnglish' was the favourite epithet. There was something inveterately continental, unmanly, underhand about Roman Catholics more especially their priests, they said. Newman himself was capable of talking in the English way on the subject. 'I wish these R.C. priests had not so smooth a manner,' he would protest, 'it puts me out'. In 1840 he could write in the *British Critic* 'We Englishmen like manliness, openness, consistency, truth . . . ' Charles Kingsley was not alone in calling him a humbug. 'Newman is doubtless a humbug,' Fitgerald declared in the following year, but he recalled that Plato had said that all wise governors may lie a little, seasonably. He was talking about Tract XC in 1841. Fitgerald had a deep-seated veneration for the Church of England, and in 1848 he drew up a petition to Lord John Russell more in sorrow than in anger at the Pope's recent creation of a Roman Hierarchy in England. Rather than submit to dishonest fooling with the words of the Liturgy and Rubric of the Church of England, (which is obviously what he thought that Newman had been doing in Tract XC) he would beg that such words be removed. In other words, let the Church of England reform herself by purifying her Liturgy of all words which lent themselves to manipulation at the hands of foolish and designing men. He had the petition printed and sent copies to his friends, but no one knows whether he secured signatures or sent it to Lord John. For the rest, he was content with a certain gentle jesting. Unlike Mr Gladstone, Fitzgerald mocked not unkindly at the High Church goings-on of his sister. 'Isabelle,' he wrote, 'has become a great Oxford Divine: she attends matins, vigils, etc. but she does not fast, which would do her more good than anything'. After all, it was not the ancient Catholic ritual that most Englishmen objected to but to being ruled by parsons, especially parsons who insisted on being called 'Priests'. The whole of the Oxford Movement, Geoffrey Faber said, 'was, in effect, a passionate assertion that the Church must rule or society cease to be Christian'. Few Englishmen have been able for long to maintain that the two positions are in fact alternatives, for they long ago discovered that the worst thing, not only for the laity, but for the Church itself, was to allow the Church to be run by the clergy. That, in a nutshell, was what the Oxford Movement was about.

Thomas Carlyle, who understood so much about his country and England, used to talk sarcastically about people who, like Coleridge 'would say and print of the Church of England with its singular old rubrics and surplices at Allhallowtide, *Esto perpetua*'. Perhaps he came from the wrong side of the Border to apprehend the truth of the matter. For all his fine achievement as a historian, he never understood that the English who lived under Queen Victoria were in essentials very much like the English who lived under Elizabeth. At least, this goes for the early Victorians. In their exuberance and facility, a late Victorian* has said, the earlier Victorians, with their flowing and scented hair, their gleaming jewellery and their resplendent waistcoats, were nearer to the later Elizabethans, especially in their sense of the worthwhileness of everything—themselves, their age, and their country. It was an age when not only did brides swoon at the altar and Ministers sometimes weep at the Communion-table, but when the sight of an infant-school could reduce a civil servant to a passion of tears . . . It was an age of flashing eyes and curling lips, an age ready to spurn, to flaunt, to admire, above all to preach.† Only in such an age could the Oxford Movement come about. And when the age was over, so was the Oxford Movement. Tract 90 was the last of the ninety. The silvery voice was still, and the great leader

*The late G. M. Young was born when the Queen had still 19 years to reign.
†Much of this paragraph comes from G. M. Young's *Early Victorian England.* Too much of it is his to make it convenient to put in quotation-marks.

had entered upon his long years of obscurity to end beneath a Cardinal's hat. The author of *Eminent Victorians* chose Manning for the first of his quartet of essays, and Newman leaves the stage less than three-quarters of the way through it. Nevertheless, it is he who enjoys the author's equivocal immortality.

CHAPTER 15

Schoolmasters and Socialists

'How do you like the Vestiges of Creation?' Edward Fitzgerald asked Bernard Barton in a letter from Brighton at Christmas, 1844. 'Are you all turned infidels—or atheists . . . ?' One didn't think much about such things down at Brighton. One's thoughts were quite enough occupied with the 'phenomenon of living with the roaring unsophisticated ocean on one side and four miles length of idle, useless, ornamental population on the other'. Like most Englishmen, he couldn't 'hold out the heroic long', which meant that generally he had to come out half-way through even the noblest rendering of *Messiah*. 'Let me plant cabbages, was the well-considered prayer of Panurge; and it is rather mine.' However, it was at pleasant Brighton and other delightful sea-side places that the Victorians became familiar with the Vestiges of Creation, in other words—Fossils.

Even before the Tractarian Movement began, to be precise, in 1830, Charles Lyell's *Principles of Geology*, was published. This great book demolished Archbishop Usher's chronology, which dated the Creation to the year 4,004 B.C., and thereby the work of Charles Darwin was made possible. For Darwin said that the science of geology was more indebted to Lyell than to any other man who ever lived. But the publication of his great book, it was said, made no more noise in the clerical world of Oxford than an explosion on the moon. The English public in general, was going through a fit of enthusiasm for popular science, of which geology was the most attractive and easy branch to come within the reach of the common man. 'The Archives of the earth,' as they were called could be ransacked by any man or woman who could afford a small hammer for rock-tapping, and knew how to read a geological map. The middle class was undergoing that craze for the collection of specimens which had swept the Paris of Louis XIV. Everyone knew Mr Tennant's shop in the Strand which was the haunt of all who wished to cultivate that 'favourite science of the day—geology'. An Englishman's parlour or library, could hardly pretend to be the habitation of a literate citizen unless it contained its 'cabinet of Specimens'. Books for infants taught them the age of the rocks and their wonderful varieties, in the form of dialogues. Magazines and reviews carrying learned geological articles could be and were bought on book-stalls. The clergy, counterparts of the French abbés, or of the comtesses who presided over the Salons of Paris, were among the pupils of whom the Keeper of the Ashmolean took account in 1870.

Two favourite habits of the Victorian family catered happily for the yearly sea-side holiday, and the pursuit of geology. The railway train carrying whole families of holiday-makers, passed through railway-cuttings which had indeed opened up the archives of the earth to their happy and studious eyes, they were like museum galleries, their varied strata arranged like display-cases to be stared at without harm to the feet. At the journey's end, were the rocks of the sea-shore at West country resorts, like Lyme Regis, and the no less happy fisherfolk, who knew where to find and sell the very best specimens. It encouraged these happy amateur families, but it was perilous stuff they were playing with, encouraging them to quarrel with Holy Writ about the Flood, the veracity of Moses, and finally the dating of Creation. The great René Descartes believed that God would never deceive René Descartes, and now here He was hiding the fossils and their testimony in unsuspected places, and making it difficult for religious men to believe in His veracity.

As the Rev. Charles Kingsley said when he read Philip Henry Gosse's *Omphalos,* which a Plymouth Brother among the naturalists published more than two years before *Darwin's Origin of the Species,* in a mistaken attempt to save the Book of Genesis from the geologists: 'I cannot give up the painful and slow conclusion of five and twenty years study of geology; I could not believe that God had written on the rocks one enormous and superfluous lie for all mankind.' He must have set a trap for naughty geologists. On the other hand, Dr Arnold thought Lyell's *Vestiges* an over-rated book and did not worry. There was no danger of it or any other geological books turning Arnold of Rugby into an atheist, with all its painful consequences—as the impious Fitz had suggested, whatever extravagances it might lead to with the eccentric Mr Gosse. To entertain the suggestion of *Omphalos* that the Maker of Heaven and Earth had deposited fossils in unlikely places as a way of testing man's faith in the Book of Genesis, was an extravagance no less insulting to God than to atheism itself. Of course there were always some people who were willing to believe anything, rather than show insufficient respect for the Almighty. 'Credo quia impossible', was a medieval attitude, sacred to John Henry Newman, whose earliest memory was a childhood wish that the Arabian Night's Tales were true . . . In the unlikely supposition that he were a member of Henry Gosse's conventicle, he would have believed his dreadful thesis.

There is only one reference to Newman's travelling by that geologically instructive vehicle the railway-train, and then he was on his way to Birmingham where he was to spend long and wretched years of exile for the sake of his True Church. From the train-window he gazed back at the medieval towers of Oxford. Dr Arnold, however, enjoyed watching the trains go past Rugby. 'I rejoice to see it', the great Headmaster is reported to have said as he peeped over the wall at the new phenomenon. 'I think it marks the end of feudality forever.' Arnold represented the Broad Church, the central tradition which eschewed both the Puritanism of the Evangelicals and fopperies of the High Church, with its Roman trappings. But then, as Cardinal Newman once asked: 'Is Dr Arnold a Christian?'

Arnold's work in his age was to take the self-consciousness of the English gentry, benevolently authoritative, but uneasily aware that its authority was waning, and give it a renewal of life by instilling into it an invaluable sense of its religious and historic justification. As one of his pupils at Rugby wrote: 'He made us think of the politics of Israel, Greece, and Rome'. The men he taught to think thus were the men of whom it has been said, and with little exaggeration, that they could, even as schoolboys, govern a whole province of the Empire at the head of a platoon of English redcoats. Arnold prolonged the rule of the English

gentry for another century beyond 1842 when it seemed to be
on its last legs. In that year he died of *angina pectoris* at the age
of 46.

It used to be said, quite inaccurately, that he tried to turn out
'The Christian Gentleman'. Men—and Christians, yes, but he was
too good a theologian, and too well-versed in human nature, to
imagine that there is such a thing as a Christian boy. Even to
suppose that in the Rugby of his régime he created 'the Public
School image' would be rash, to say the least, but he did depend
greatly upon his Prefects and his Sixth Form. He did, too, lay a
great deal more emphasis on character than is tolerable to later
generations which like to imagine that he was the inventor of
compulsory games, which he certainly was not. He has been made
to bear responsibility for many things that little men have come
to detest. To resort to the silly jargon of a later age, Arnold 'got
his priorities right'. He once said that intellectual acuteness
divested of all that is comprehensive and great and good, is 'more
revolting than the most helpless imbecility'. In that kind of remark he was re-iterating Coleridge's contempt for 'shop-boy
sharpness' as the concomitant of intellect. Power resulting from
the acquisition of knowledge and skill, or the superior develop-
ment of the understanding, Coleridge had taught him, was no
doubt of a superior kind to the mere physical strength and fierce-
ness of a beast, but it needed to be combined with and guarded by
the moral qualities of prudence, industry, and self-control if it
were not to result in the tyranny of an 'aristocracy of talent'.

Dr Arnold represented the Broad Church Movement most
directly and importantly in his concern for the Church as the
comprehensive reflection of a Christian society, rather than as the
guardian of a theology, a hierarchy, or its endowments. To Arnold
the important differences between men were not those between
Church and Chapel, between High and Low, but between
Christian and non-Christian. He was among the first to realise that
the churchman's problem was not the upholding of the Apostolic
Succession, which he said seemed to be 'almost the only subject
insisted upon in the two first volumes of *The Tracts for the Times*,
1833–1836'. This, and the consequent exclusive claims of the
Church of England to be regarded as the only true church *in*

England, if not in the world. He never went so far as to say that he thought such pre-occupations in the fourth decade of the 19th century were frivolous, but he plainly thought that 'the one doctrine which was then put forward by the High Church as the cure for the moral and social evils of the country' was morally powerless and intellectually indefensible, incompatible with all sound notions of law and government, tending above all to substitute a ceremonial for a spiritual Christianity.

Not the Apostolical Succession, not the dangers of Schism or Disendowment, but the advance of forces which threatened the very existence of religion in the semi-barbarous society of industrial England: that was, or should have been, the principal concern of Christian men. The Established Church had for too long been compromised as a possible agent of social justice by its alliance with the aristocracy. It was identified in the popular mind with the forces of conservatism, the defence of the *status quo*. Lord Acton called the Church in the France of the *ancien régime* 'the gilded crutch of the Monarchy'. When the revolution began in 1789, the lower clergy in general stood by the *Tiers Etat*. After all, the average *curé* was a peasant in a cassock. In England, the same line-up of clergy and democracy was problematical, often quite beyond imagining. Some of the best-hated figures of the world of William Cobbett were the 'Squarsons', the Parson-magistrates, people like Parson Hay who was for twenty years Chairman of the Manchester and Salford bench of magistrates, the efficient organizer of an information or spy service, the self-constituted permanent police-magistrate for the West Riding of Yorkshire. Another was Robert Lowe, the hunting 'squarson' of Bingham in Nottingham, father of a more famous Robert Lowe who was to play a disastrous part in the history of elmentary education by initiating the iniquitous 'Payment by Results' system. The Rev. Robert Lowe put much faith in what was called 'the wholesome terror of the Workhouse', as he said, in 1818, as a way of lowering the Poor Rates. There were a great many others of these 'Black Dragoons', to use Cobbett's term. Indeed their numbers were on the increase, as a correspondent observed in writing to the Home Office in 1817. After all if Thomas Arnold and his heroes were right about the identity of Church and State, was this to be wondered at, let alone deplored? All the same, the 'squarson' remained the least acceptable character in rural, or even provincial England.

What, however, of the 'Christian-Socialist' party? It was by no means inevitable that the Anglican clergy should always be 'Under-strappers of the landed aristocracy', though it was not surprising that they were such, considering that the rural parson was often a younger brother of the squire, so that the term 'squire-and-parson' was for long thought to be a natural, inevitable, and desirable conjunction. Arnold himself, however, set an example of different sympathies. He was, if not a Radical, at least a Liberal. 'I do not think I am democratically inclined', he wrote to J. T. Coleridge in 1817, 'and God forbid I should ever be such a clergyman as Horne Tooke.' Like his son, Matthew, he was deeply impressed by the effects of the cult of equality in France. Indeed when he was in France in 1839, he wrote home about the ease of intercourse between rich and poor. Like most Englishmen he hoped this might mean a 'levelling up' rather than a 'levelling down', adding 'though I do not believe that I am an aristocrat, yet I should grieve beyond measure if our standard of morals or of manners were to be lowered'. If Old England were to perish as Old France had perished at the Revolution there would perish not 'a mere accursed thing, such as was the system of Old France', but 'the most active and noble life which the world has ever yet seen'.

It was high time that the National Church stopped crying that 'The Church was in danger', and substituted some such cry as 'The Poor are Perishing'. The two were closely related, for the poor would care for the church, only in so far as the Church cared for them. In the 1830's it became alarmingly clear not only that (as Coleridge had said) 'the Church has let the hearts of the common people be stolen from it', but that religion itself was coming to mean very little to the poor—and perhaps not much more to the rich, except as an insurance policy. When the great inter-denominational struggle to win control of the schools for the children of the poor was raging in the 'forties and 'fifties, some one observed sardonically that while one party was frightened that the little children would grow up as little Anglicans, and the other that they would grow up as little Dissenters, the children were actually growing up as little heathens.

To win back a godless people, to talk about 'Church-Unity', was not enough; Ecumenical movements then, as now, have been little more than a papering over the cracks. Only the National Church, as Arnold and the 'Broad Churchmen' learnt its nature from Coleridge, could embody the nation in such a way that the Bible became, as he called it in the title of his most famous essay, or first Lay Sermon 'The Statesman's Manual'. People imagined that the poet was proposing to consult the Scriptures like a Fundamentalist or a dealer in Prophecy, because he was unwise enough to adopt a sub-title reminiscent of Old Moore's Almanac: 'The Bible the Best Guide to Policial Skill and Foresight', and to add an Appendix 'containing Comments and Essays connected with the Study of the Inspired Writings'. In fact, the sense in which Coleridge recommended the Bible as a guide or manual, was the sense in which the Bible is History, not the 'cause-and-effect' History of Michelet or Macaulay or Marx, but a prophetic symbolism which yields a science of realities as only the Bible can. The Bible interpreted by 'science, scholarship, and above all by political insight', was History robbed of its accidentality and Science robbed of its fatalism, indeed the record of a redemptive process in action.

This view of the Bible and of the Church led some frightened people, like Newman, to ask 'Is Dr Arnold a Christian?', just as it had once led them to ask it about Coleridge himself, suspecting that he was some kind of German Transcendentalist. Arnold at least, knew better than that. 'I think with all his faults old Sam was more of a great man than any one who has lived within the four seas in my memory,' he once reported. It was Coleridge's opinion that while there should be no party politics in the pulpit, 'every church in England should ring with national politics'. When he heard men talk of 'The Church', Arnold said, he could not help recalling how the Abbé Sièyes replied to the question 'What is the Tiers Etat?' by saying that it was '*La nation moins la noblesse et le clergé*'. So, if he were asked 'What is the laity?' he would answer, 'The Church minus the clergy'. Unfortunately, he added, the Oxford malignants (which was his term for the Oxford

Movement, in general) meant by the Church the clergy, the hierarchy exclusively, which Arnold called their 'first and fundamental
apostasy'. He was reluctant even to talk of an alliance or union of
Church and State, for they were not two societies, but one, and
only in proportion as this identity was realised could man's perfection and God's glory be established on earth. This was the
theory sanctioned by some of the greatest names in English
theology and philosophy, by Hooker, by Burke, and in part by
Coleridge.

To Thomas Arnold, 'Church Reform' meant comprehension,
and first of all the comprehending of the Dissenters within the
pale of the Establishment. If this meant the use of different forms
of worship at different hours of the Sunday in the parish Church,
thus it must be. Such an indifference to dogma horrified the
'malignants' in Arnold's time, as it horrified a Roman Catholic
like Ronald Knox a hundred years later as evidenced in his satirical
essay, 'Reunion all round'. Even Thomas Carlyle could issue a
grimly ironical warning against Dean Stanley, who was Arnold's
pupil and first biographer: 'There's that Dean down in the hold,
bore,—bore,—boring, and some day he'll bore through and let
all the water in'. It was Disraeli who warned the Dean, 'No dogma
—no Dean!' Queen Victoria, who hated having Bishops to tea
and always went off on a country carriage-drive when they had
gone, made Stanley her favourite Dean. After all, a truly national
character like a Queen, had to be 'Broad'.

The Broad-church movement produced Christian Socialism.
When Max Beer wrote his *History of British Socialism* which was
published in English more than fifty years ago, he opened it with
a lengthy account of its Christian origins, and it is true that
Socialism in England took its rise within the ethics and the philosophy of Christianity. It bears its birth-marks not only in the
communistic sentiment of medieval men of action like the peasant
leader, John Ball, and the late medieval humanism of Thomas
More, but in the poetry and poetising of the Romantic poets. Two
revolutions gave it great volition, the French and the Industrial.
If the French Revolution was a scourge, the poets decided, it was
at any rate 'le fleau de Dieu', God's chastisement of man on
account of his inhumanity to man, a view expressed by M. Charles

Cestre; as for the Industrial Revolution, a brief diagnosis is to be found in Disraeli's grim utterance—'Only Christian institutions can humanize Manchester'. It was, however, not until 1848 that two clergymen proclaimed themselves Christian Socialists. They were Frederick Denison Maurice, who was Professor of Divinity at King's College, London, and Charles Kingsley, the muscular-Christian Rector of Eversley in Devon, soon to become a highly popular and successful Victorian novelist. A layman closely associated with them was Tom Hughes, the celebrated author of *Tom Brown's Schooldays*. Maurice was the life-long disciple of Coleridge, although oddly enough his father was a Unitarian minister who quaintly baptised children 'in the name of the Father, the Son and the Holy Ghost', which meant someone said, that he baptised them in the name of an abstraction, a man and a metaphor. May this help to account for Maurice's combination of extreme saintliness with utter ineffectiveness on paper?

The Christian Socialists of the Broad-church taught that Socialism was Christianity in action, an instance of the naïveté which captivates the youthful idealist and repels the 'man of the world' who lives in every working politician if only because it is in the world that he has to work. There were the prototypes of the schoolmaster or the young don who sets his pupils essay-subjects like 'Was Jesus Christ a pacifist?' or (as a French exercise) 'Platon, est-il Fasciste?' Nevertheless they lighted a candle that has never been, and probably never will be, put out, as a variety of Socialism. Their weekly paper, *Politics for the People*, had the explicit purpose of showing that politics had been for too long kept separate from Christianity, and they were fond of attributing the failure of the Socialism of Robert Owen to his repudiation of Christianity. 'The People' for whom they produced their politics have never shown more than a fitful enthusiasm for their journalism, in much the same way that the Socialist Party is normally rejected by the people at the polls when it proclaims itself 'The People's Party'. The English people do not like to be called 'the People' just as the Englishman hates to be called 'the Common Man'. For one thing, he attaches a slighting connotation to the adjective 'common'. He belongs to an aristocratic tradition.

CHAPTER 16

Happy Ending?

ONE OF the most distinguished examples of 'doodling' on record was that perpetrated by Joseph Paxton on a piece of blotting-paper at a Board-meeting of the Directors of the Midland Railway in the station-hotel, Derby. It has been preserved, that pen-and ink sketch of the great glass-house which won the prize for an Exhibition building to house the transient glories of early Victorian Britain in Hyde Park in 1851. Joseph Paxton had become head-gardener at Chatsworth, 'The Palace of the Peak,' at the age of twenty, a notable example—as Queen Victoria said—of the Career open to Talent, a social phenomenon no less notable in railway history than in Napoleonic. It was only by unhappy chance that a £25,000 monument to George Hudson, the Railway King, was not set up at Hyde Park Corner, a consummation devoutly to be wished by a great commercial nation, as Thomas Carlyle argued in a savagely satirical essay in 1850. The cast-iron image of this 'Incarnation of the English Vishnu', as Carlyle called it, should have been mounted on a metal model of a loco-motive, garnished with 'Scrip-rolls proper', ten tons of brass to serve as brass portrait of King Hudson mounted above the busiest thoroughfare of the English world. This would have been the apotheosis of the successful linen-draper of York, while another brazen image at Swindon might have memorialised the successful commercial career of Sir Daniel Gooch, the Chairman of the Great Western Railway. It was Daniel Gooch's mother who had de-lighted Matthew Arnold by her version of the Golden Rule, whereby she kept before young Daniel's eyes throughout his youth the admonition to the virtuous apprentice: 'Ever remember, my dear Dan, that you should look forward to being someday the manager of that concern!' Perhaps Joseph Paxton's prize-winning design for what became 'The Crystal Palace' in Hyde Park might serve as a memorial for them all, although that 'Alp of Glass,' in Martin Tupper's image, was destroyed by fire when it was later removed to the heights of Sydenham, and example of delayed nemesis, for had not Col. Sibthorpe predicted, indeed prayed in Parliament that the Divine Wrath would fall upon the godless structure while it was still in course of construction?

Paxton had won the prize in competition with more than two hundred and fifty others from all over the world. His design was adapted from that of the Lily-house conservatory he had begun to build for the Duke of Devonshire at Chatsworth in year of the Queen's accession. The use of glass in an iron frame was a stroke of genius, for glass had become a great deal cheaper in recent years with the removal of tariffs. What more suitable than a glass-house to exhibit the products of Free Trade? There was something magical and fairy-like about it too.

> As though 'twere by a wizard's rod,
> A blazing arch of lucid glass
> Leaps like a fountain from the grass
> To meet the sun.

'The crystal palace' was nearly two thousand feet long and some four hundred feet wide, and constructed of standard lengths of iron and glass so that any part could be simply and easily replaced. With its galleries and transepts it was the nineteenth-century counterpart of the medieval cathedral, celebrating the English deity of material progress. Not everyone was enraptured by it. John Ruskin thought it monstrous that people gave artistic significance to 'a greenhouse larger than ever greenhouse was built before', or boasted about 'an entirely novel order of architecture,' though even he was prepared to admit the ingenuity of a pre-fabricated structure of cast-iron pillars and plate-glass panels. William Morris, however, cast himself down on a seat in Hyde Park in a fainting condition at the sight of such a 'monstrosity' in the land of Chaucer and Shakespeare. 'The British lower public,' Ruskin wrote, 'has no very clear notion of the way to amuse itself,' it has a notion of improving its manners and getting useful information at the same time, and so makes its way to the Crystal Palace, and with its own instincts principally tending towards ginger-beer, hopes also to have its mind enlarged by the assistance of Greek sculpture, always supposing the enlargement of its mind is to tend somehow to the enlargement of pockets, wages, and other substantialities. . . . '

The Prince Consort presided over the enterprise. 'Paxton, go forth,' Mr Punch represented the Prince saying to the gardener, 'take glass and iron, and, beauty wedding strength, produce the Industrial Hall of Nations.' For the Crystal Palace was dedicated, above all else, to the Peace and Brotherhood of Nations. *Paxton vobiscum* was Mr Punch's felicitous pun. And should not the emblematic tree of the Great Exhibition be the olive? After all, one of the things that chiefly delighted many of the visitors was the fact that some of the trees of Hyde Park were actually enclosed within the great glass-house, a fact which at first raised some backward thoughts about the droppings of the sparrows, to the detriment of the exhibits, until the Duke of Wellington produced his celebrated advice to the Queen: 'Sparrowhawks, Ma'am! Sparrowhawks!'

The other thing that caused much apprehension, apart from the sparrows, was the foreigners, large numbers of whom were expected to flock into the capital, many of them no doubt being thieves and even anarchists. Quite apart from the foreigners, there was the fear which had haunted Government for many years that large assemblages of working-class people would turn into revolutionary gatherings. No doubt the situation would afford an admirable opportunity for Sir Robert Peel's metropolitan police to prove their worth. All the same, large-scale disorder, even revolution was prophesied, And it was attempted to persuade the Queen not to drive through the streets on the opening day. The Queen herself, however, was not to be deterred, and the day passed off in great good-humour and the smell of current-buns and ginger-beer. From that day forth, it is said, the British Monarchy has always felt itself safest, and happiest, in the midst of the people of the capital. The Queen and her family drove to the opening on 1st May in open carriages (amidst scenes of great enthusiasm) with no more than the customary sovereign's escort of Household Cavalry. There were no soldiers, and hardly a policeman in sight that day. Twenty-five thousand people turned out to watch, and all through that splendid summer the daily average was 43,000, six million in all. Large numbers were carried cheaply to London by excursion trains, so that the people who had made the exhibits and the Crystal Palace itself were able at once to participate in the triumphs. There was a general spirit of fraternity, perfect strangers stopped and shook hands, even with 'foreigners', and everyone said that the conduct of people was exemplary. They consumed three million buns and a million bottles of mineral-water. No intoxicants were on sale. But the crowds began by joining in the rendering of the *Allelujah Chorus* by the massed-choirs, and continued to sing *God save the Queen* at the slightest provocation throughout the proceedings. Sadly, the weather turned wet in the last days.

What did this gigantic and solemn rejoicing stand for? It may be said to have symbolised the unification of England after the long years of alarm and rancour which had dominated the social relationships of industrial England for at least a generation. Karl Marx was already spending laborious days in the British Museum Reading-room, that great and quiet forcing-house of the revolution that never came. He never failed in respect and admiration of the great productive achievement of British capitalism symbolised in Hyde Park in 1851, even while he deplored its distributive injustices. No doubt he likewise deplored the evidence the Exhibition may have afforded of the easing of the class war on which his doctrine of revolution depended, in other words that the story which had opened at Peterloo seemed at last to be heading towards a happy, if Victorian, ending.

Index